The Wal-Mart Chronicles and Other Stories

by

J. C. Kradel

THE WAL-MART CHRONICLES & OTHER STORIES

JOSEPH KRADEL
BLEAK HUMOR BOOKS

ISBN # 978-0-578-00793-9

FOR –

TK, Fletch, Kiki, Boo, and Maddog

Authors Note:

Outside of the accomplishments of actual Arkansas sports figures I have taken quite a few liberties with the facts. While there are characters in these stories that resemble my family and friends and people that cross my path at work, I have actually made up all the folks in these pages. My real life isn't funny enough to put down on paper.

Table of Contents

The Wal-Mart Chronicles

Soft Core

(A Wal-Mart Chronicle)

Part One

I have a strange relationship with Wal-Mart. I despise the place yet I find myself undeniably drawn to her. (And make no mistake, Wal-Mart is a female - a siren of sorts) Standing outside her doors at two o'clock in the morning after swearing I would never come back, I feel like some sort of stalker ex-boyfriend. It reminds me in a weird way of the 2000 presidential elections when Bush was stealing the recount in Florida. Katherine Harris was all over the news pretending to be impartial and always standing in profile, her back arched carefully. She was awful and frightening and tacky and improperly medicated and embodied everything that was wrong with the world just then but there was no doubt in my mind that I wanted to sleep with her. A part of me was strangely desperate to suckle at her ample silicone teat. In many ways this is how I feel about Wal-Mart.

I told that story to a female therapist once and asked her what it meant. She said she thought I would be better off with a male therapist and that I made her very uncomfortable with my use of the word "teat". My problems with Wal-Mart have continued.

The inspiration for this foray into the mouth of the beast was, as usual, late night television. I was eating a box of cinnamon Pop Tarts, smoking cigarettes, reading a book and maybe, just maybe, perusing the net for some Latin American midget amputee porn. The TV was on just to keep the voices in my head quiet. The soothing light and rhythmic cadences that flicker from the box calm my inner static.

For some reason I noticed an infomercial for a Bowflex that I had seen a million times before. The female model was ripped - simply fantastic in that perky, personal trainer kind of way. It occurred to me in that moment, as I was brushing Pop Tart and ash off my lap, that in my current state of fitness I would never again sleep with a woman that good looking, or even aspire to sleep with a woman that good looking. I simply had to start working out again, if only to keep some sense of realism in my masturbatory fantasies.

It seemed to me that all of these workout shows and commercials had suddenly started focusing on the "core". This was a term that had cropped up in the last couple of years and had immediately become ubiquitous. They used these BIG RUBBER BALLS to stabilize "the core". The used a trampoline to focus on "the core". It seemed as if they sort of meant the abs but were including the back, the intestines and possibly even feces as well. Regardless of its meaning, if any human being ever needed work on his "core" it was me. My core was soft and weak. It lacked definition both in actuality and in theory. I was off to Wal-Mart at 2 a.m. to buy a big rubber ball.

I should have turned around when the greeter looked at me with pinpoint pupils, said "NO WAY", horse laughed, pulled me in for a smoky hug, and laid a kiss on my cheek that squished with old lady tongue. Things tended to be a bit different at this Wal-Mart.

The greeter was named Wanda and, at 67, she is perhaps the oldest meth-head that I know. At least she is the oldest FEMALE tweaker. There is a three generational family of crank cooks up near Oark that haven't slept since '91, haven't a tooth among them and exist on baby food, tater tots, and milk shakes, that I run into every so often at the Sonic that might have her beat. The patriarch of that clan must be 75.

Wanda has been clean, as far as I know, for about 3 years but she still pops into the ER quite a bit because she likes pills. She likes pills a lot. Somehow she had managed to pass a pre-employment drug screen and here she was at Wal-Mart.

She was in a motorized cart with her right ankle in a cast. A fall at work that day had broken her left ankle. Unfortunately Wal-Mart and Tyson have both threatened our hospital and a couple of local doctors with pulling all of their patients and contracts if their worker's comp injuries are given ANY time off at all unless the patients are actively bleeding to death. Apparently it helps their insurance rates to have the injured back on the job doing "light duty". So Wanda is back at work with a smashed right ankle the same day she broke it, giddy on Vicodin, and chasing people around on her Rascal.

"You look fat, Doc. Hey, you want one of these? They gave me a bunch. Pretty soothing." She held out a handful of pills. Now this is the sort of greeting we need at more retail establishments.

I passed on the pills, as much because they came from her grubby pocket as anything else. I waved to her and wiped her slobber from my cheek.

The aisles seem blessedly empty at first but this proves to be an illusion. A Wal-Mart at 2a.m. is alive with people filled with purpose. Two guys with scabby facial hair are having a slap fight over a floor polisher. A lady I know with a thicker mustache than either of them tries to flirt with each of these fellows in turn. A couple of guys that look like they might be fleeing parole are skulking in the oversized lingerie section, eyeing really big bras. A tank topped woman who weighs in somewhere near 300 pounds pushes a cart wearily. Her 2 shirtless children, their faces smeared with kool-aid, buzz around in a sugar fueled mania, touching everything in sight with grubby fingernails. Everyone seems oblivious to the time.

A few years ago almost all Wal-Marts added grocery stores. They call them "Supercenters" but I'm not sure they have just "regular centers" any more. I can't even remember what it was like in the days before I could do my grocery shopping at the same time I'm picking up a giant rubber exercise ball and maybe some windshield wiper fluid and perhaps ,if I think about it, a large knife . I feel sorry for any town with just a a "regular center". I shall surely mock them if I ever drive through such a place.

So for some reason I find myself in the freezer section. Not really just for some reason. It started out because I was dodging the fat lady and her dirty children and then I saw a splinter group of the Clayton clan. (The Claytons are a family that it seems I met my first day working in the ER here about 10 years ago and I have been trying unsuccessfully to avoid them ever since. They are innumerable and seemingly quite fertile. At one point they were in some sort of dirty-families-with-no-visible-means-of-support alliance with the Osters from the other side of the hill but there had been some sort of falling out over a sofa, a dirty t-shirt, a tool box, and a comely lass who suffered from partial facial paralysis and couldn't blink her left eye. The whole thing ended in in a near brawl that was only averted because everyone was in such horrible health they couldn't manage to fight. Several ambulances were called to haul the coughing, wheezing, back clutching bunch to the ER. I could go on for days about the Claytons so I'll stop there and just say that I was trying to dodge them.)

Cool temperatures and ice cream seemed the opposite of scratchy, dirty people so it was to the freezer section I went. This did little to harden up my soft core. I LOVE the freezer section. The possibilities are endless and the air is cold and sterile. There are popsicles and pies and frozen enchiladas that look wonderful in the picture but don't work out so good when you get them home - much like many women in my life. And there is Ben and Jerry's, where I stop to kneel and pray.

Having sung praises to my heroes of softness I grabbed a tub of Creme Brulee and, as I turned to start down the aisle, I received my second unsolicited hug of the night. I badly needed another place to shop.

It was Lucy and she ALWAYS hugs me. Every single time she sees me. Anywhere. Anytime. She is a hugger Lucy is. It defines her. Much in the way NOT being a hugger defines ME.

She loves me. She claims I found her tumor. She tells everybody this. It isn't true. I had, in fact, become so frustrated by NEVER finding anything wrong with this enormous, vertiginous, vomiting woman that I sent her to someone else who very quickly DID find the problem which was a benign tumor in her ear. He then fixed her. At least he fixed that particular problem.

Lucy is a sweetheart but she has some issues. She was way up over 300 pounds at one point and has recently gotten a gastric bypass. It was successful, I guess, in that she has dropped 150 pounds but there were some problematic side effects.

Her stomach hurts all the time. She has chronic diarrhea. And every few minutes she retches like she is going to vomit and then spits up some phlegm-like material. She carries around a barf-bag to collect this. I'm not joking. I argued with her that at this point the retching and spitting had mostly become habit but she would just wave me off and retch and spit.

Behind Lucy is her tiny husband Donny. He is always behind her. That is his place. He is quivering. This happens from time to time. He doesn't shake or tremble. He quivers. As if at an atomic level. Almost imperceptibly. Like brownian movement. This will soon be followed by his collapsing and falling to the ground in a heap. This happens anywhere from 1 to 20 times a day. He doesn't like me and truth be told I'm not a big fan of his work either.

I nod to him in the way that men nod to each other. He tries to nod back in kind but it is hard to nod appropriately while wearing a hairnet and tiny, quivering Donny is wearing a hairnet. He wears a hairnet everywhere. The thing is that despite being small, pale, inarguably ugly, always passing out and married to a formerly fat woman who carries around a barf bag, Donny is surprisingly vain and self-important. And his frequent collapses have, in the past, led to his nicely permed blonde locks becoming dirty and lopsided. He felt this was unacceptable. Thus the hairnet.

"You look fat Doc" says Lucy, vomiting into her bag.

I shrug, unable to argue with this simple truth. "It's the ice cream", I say. "It's softening my core."

Lucy reaches into her huge purse and pulls out some ziplock bags filled with an unidentifiable meat-like substance. We hear a THUD as she hands them to me. Donny is laying quietly on the ground. We both glance briefly at him then go on with what we were doing as if total loss of motor control were a completely normal thing for us to witness.

"It's deer jerky Doc", Lucy says. "We hit a deer with the truck. Donny passed out for an hour that time. I probably shouldn't let him drive. Anyway, I'll bring some up to the hospital. And some chili. It's good for you." She pauses to retch. Donny gets to his feet and checks his hairnet. He eyes me suspiciously, as if I may have violated him while he napped.

It is an interesting fact that people with real sudden seizures or cataplexy suffer pretty severe injuries, or at least cuts and bruises, when they fall. Donny never had. He always goes down soft. It's not that he's faking so much, just maybe subconsciously. I and others have suggested this to him. This is why he doesn't like me and why he ramps up the performance whenever I am around.

I thank Lucy and wave to Donny. I get ANOTHER hug goodbye and, as I turn to resume my quest for a big rubber ball, I trip over a lurking Wanda in her Rascal, stubbing my sandaled toe.

"Dammit Wanda."

"Just wanted to make sure you were having a pleasant shopping experience" she says and pops a Vicodin.

We both turn and look as we hear Lucy retch and Donny flop to the ground.

Part Two

"My hair is falling out" says Wanda, eagerly showing me two fistfuls of her grey/black tufts. She looks up at me with her eyes wide and hopeful, as if I was a person who had answers to problems such as these.

"It's not so much falling out as you're yanking it out by the roots Wanda." I look from her scalp to the hair in her hands. Bloody specks have dried where the hair has been pulled out. Tiny bits of flesh and dandruff cling to the plugs. Fucking tweekers.

Wanda runs over my feet with her Rascal as she hurries to greet more customers. I watch her go, frail hands clutching strands of hair, casted broken foot splayed slightly to the side. Her path is drunken yet aggressive, bumping into the aisles and knocking Charmin to the ground silently. I feel suddenly alone in the vastness of the store.

I move away from groceries into housewares, leaving a small trail of blood from an injured toenail, courtesy of Wanda's Rascal. A wondrous latino girl looks at me strangely, like she knows me from somewhere and maybe likes me. She is young enough that I might have taken care of her as a child. Her eyebrows are shaved off and painted back on. Lips are outlined in black. I try to look away from her mouth but it is impossible. She says something to me in spanish and it is like I am in a dream and I am paralyzed, frozen by REM sleep, unable to respond to words I should understand. She just giggles and moves to the next aisle.

I am in Automotive now. I always like it here. It smells of rubber and grease and windex and leather and things I don't understand and could never use. It is like a foriegn country filled with serious men nodding to each other, agreeing silently on the proper tools and date rape drugs.

Sporting Goods are in sight from here. I am going to make it. Maybe.

I can hear Clay Clayton berating his one-legged brother, Eddie. I can hear Eddie crying. I am hoping they are in pharmaceuticals, maybe fighting over hygiene products, a bar of soap, a washcloth, Nix, anything. No such luck.

I spot Clay moving up the fishing aisle like something out of an Ed Wood movie. He has a stiffness and a limp that seems strange and put on, his arms slightly out in front like a monster.

His one legged brother is hopping next to him, leaving a trail of resistant twenty-second century bacteria in his wake. The leg was a long ago victim of a canine/human cross breeding experiment gone sadly awry, his persistent perirectal abscesses a source of continuing misery for us all.

Eddie starts shoving Clay and Clay wants none of it.

Eddie is the kid brother and lives in the camper section of a pick up that sits in the yard of the Clayton compound. The whole family regrets not pulling the dog off him sooner when he was a boy, so they indulge him quite a bit. They bring him whiskey, which he drinks all day every day, and food, which he doesn't eat, but it finds its way into his beard anyway, and they let him use some of his own social security money.

They had even let him play with one of the 12 year old nephews, Nate, most nights. At least until Human Services got involved because of Nate's nasty staph infections. It sounds like that is what this argument is about. Eddie wants Nate back. Clay wants him to make do with one of the hounds. Eddie is scared of dogs. And on and on. Until Clay finally just shoves Eddie backwards.

Eddie hops sideways a few times like a drunken clown on a pogo stick before crashing into display of lures. He is crying and sniffling and crawling across the floor like a snail, leaving a trail of pus as he inches along, a tiny plastic fishing lure hooked in his cheek.

Wanda motors by and tosses Clay some moist towlettes.

Clean up in aisle five please.

Part Three

The big rubber balls are across from the treadmills and the weight benches. There are basketballs and jump ropes and grip enhancers and golf clubs and tennis racquets and everything looks nice but it is all slightly cheap and off brand. Just like the very young woman sitting on the big rubber balls, making out with a guy that looks like he just got off work at the chicken plant. His hands slip in and out of the waist band of her dirty hip huggers and her half shirt exposes a core that looks like it could use some help too. Maybe that is how she ended up on the big rubber ball.

The kissing is the aggressive licking that you see at a drive-in or maybe when a drunken domestic violence couple make up and tell each other they didn't mean it. Tongues flashing and slurpy sounds. Hugs and hickeys. I should turn immediately and walk away, give up on my quest. But I am transfixed for a few seconds, mesmerized by the sights and sounds of this young pair, kind of like when you come across a bad soft porn movie on cable. You want to turn the channel but don't. Then she looks at me. She smiles shyly.

"Hey doc" she says and giggles, wiping her mouth with the back of her hand. "They let you off tonight huh.? Gettin' kinda fat aren't ya?"

Aren't we all. Ally had been 14 and pregnant the first time I saw her. Eight months along and about 100 pounds soaking wet. Her parents brought her in for a pregnancy test. I told them it wasn't necessary as you could feel the baby's head and feet quite easily.

I remember her very well because she was the only extremely pregnant 14 year old who ever hit on me.

She is in her early twenties now, has another kid. But she never really seems to have found her place in the white trash culture. She tried to do the "headache girl" thing but her heart wasn't in it. Then she tried to be the girl with dozens of kids by lots of dads getting enough checks to get by but she wasn't fertile enough. Her tubes scarred and rescarred over the years by a variety of STDs. She even tried to be a chronic back pain person on disability but that involved getting up early enough to go to the doctor all the time and she was just too lazy for that.

Lately she is trying for meth addict whore but clearly it is just a hobby for her. She simply doesn't have enough want to.

"What are you doing here doc?" Ally asks. She is nuzzling the chicken guy. They can't stop touching each other. If it wasn't so revolting it would have been sweet. He smells like rendered animal fat.

I guess I could explain. Could tell her about the Pop Tarts and my soft core. Talk about the Claytons and Lucy. It seems to not be the best idea. Things get that way at Wal-Mart. They get confused and layered and complicated. They get ugly and cheap and embarassing. "Nothing" I say. "Just getting some ice cream. What about you?"

Ally doesn't say anything either, just looks at the two boxes of Sudafed in her cart.

"So how do you guys know each other?" asks chicken guy.

Now both Ally and I kind of look at the floor, thinking of her childhood incest and pregnancy, her drips and itches, the shit I know about her that one human being should never, ever know about another and we both kind of laugh.

This is Wal-Mart to us. It is our inescapable disease and past. It is something so vast that it can never be left behind no matter what medicine we take.

I am leaving and Wanda comes by and bumps me with her shoulder. "Shouldn't hang out with trash like that doc. They're always over at my house. Drugs and all that."

"I'll keep it in mind Wanda."

She holds out her dirty little hand. "Vicodin doc?"

I shake my head and leave. I leave without my big rubber ball. Maybe I will get it next time. Or maybe my core is hopeless.

Coaches on Aisle 5

The Wal-Mart Chronicles . . .

Note: This was written during the University of Arkansas football coaching search in late 2007.

"I do have some young coaches, but I don't really believe that is the biggest problem we have here."

Steve Spurrier- discussing South Carolina football

It was midnight and I was bored so I went to Wal-Mart to see if they had any football coaches. I couldn't find any. Who knows, they might just be sold out. Christmas rush and all.

There was a gray haired lady with big glasses sitting on her butt restocking Milkduds. I asked her if she knew where I could find any coaches. She sighed and told me to try Aisle 5.

Aisle 5 didn't have any coaches. Unless the 300 pound 18 year old hispanic kid who had his underwear hanging out and his crack showing while he was bobbing his head to the irregular beat of something on his headphones was a coach. He might have been but I didn't think Razorback Nation was ready for him.

Aisle 5 DID have granola bars and Pop Tarts. I really like Brown Sugar Cinnamon Pop Tarts but the fat guy with the headphones seemed to be guarding them so I threw a box of Frosted Flakes on the floor to distract him while I grabbed two boxes. That's how a coach thinks, you see. Strategically.

Over in Guns & Ammo was a guy who wore a lot of denim, had a greasy trucker cap and was comparing the sharpness of a series of very large knives. His belt buckle said his name was Alvin but we all know that belt buckles can't be trusted. Alvin looked like the kind of guy that could lead me to the coaches, be they alive or dead. So I asked my question. It turned out that denim clad, greasy guys looking at knives don't like to be approached by strange men asking weird questions in Wal-Mart. Luckily security knows me there.

I decided to get a movie, since it's tough to be alone in Arkansas without a football coach, but even the DVD's I bought seemed to be omens of the search, "Superbad" and "Pirates of the Caribbean: At World's End".

The Wal-Mart Chronicles . . .

I looked in Sporting Goods and Home Improvement. I searched in Menswear and spent an inappropriate amount of time in the plus-size lingerie section. No coaches there. I did find a Matt Jones doll. In Jaguars gear no less. Collectors item.

It was 2am by now and I was thinking it was time to be giving up my search. Only one register was open and I joined the scraggly crew that shops at the same time I do in line.

At the front of the line there was a middle aged guy wearing a Razorback sweatshirt with the sleeves cut off. His left arm was amputated at mid bicep and I had to look twice to be sure I wasn't imagining it. He was flexing his stump as he tried to put a box under his bad wing. The scar tissue pulled taut then loosened. It looked foreign and out of place and its movement was mesmerizing.

As he left an older lady, probably 70, with a bluish tint to her hair and slippers on her feet had her items slide through the scanner. She was buying a Razorback seat cushion, Marlboro Reds, condoms, candles, and a Daughtry CD. I thought the musical selection was odd.

Right in front of me was a young couple. They were maybe 21 and tweeking so hard they were practically vibrating. Buying cigarettes, gum, and juice. Rattling on in unintelligible bursts about LSU and high school coaches and 3 overtimes and the greatest game they had ever seen.

Outside the air was crisp and cool. White lights silhouetted large houses on the hill overlooking the parking lot. Bells, real and imagined, were ringing in my head. There is a feel to the Christmas season and tonight had it.

But Razorback Nation is lonely this Christmas. It is confused and depressed and nearing psychosis. We need a football coach. Or things might start to get weird.

Stripper Story

(A Wal-Mart Chronicle)

The Wal-Mart Chronicles . . .

"Yeah I'm telling real stories,but if you pick up a documentary on strippers, you're going to want some stripping, so we definitely got that in there."

Method Man

A stripper called me the other day. Called me at my house. I'm serious. The phone rang and I checked the caller ID, the name and number didn't ring a bell so I answered.

"Hey there, it's your future ex-wife" , a semi-smoky voice said. These are the sorts of things that happen to me. And for some reason they always lead to Wal-Mart.

Why a stripper would have my home number and why she would be calling me are perfectly good questions, but the complete answers probably wouldn't fit in this space. Let me just start by saying that I used to have a few problems. Maybe that should just sum it up for now.

I recognized her voice and even remembered her name, sort of. Her professional name was Blue and her real name was Elizabeth or something like that. She also had a web name, I think it was Joe, but I had never used it so it didn't wear a notch in my brain. I never knew what to call her and I'm not sure she knew what to call herself. She used opening lines like the "future ex-wife" bit. Things get sketchy when a stripper and her patron lose their context.

We chatted for a few moments, like old school chums or something. I asked about her job and she asked about mine. She sounded okay if a little bit flighty, maybe a bit harried. "Can you come over and look at my leg? I hurt it and can't afford to go to the doctor."

I said that I would and after checking that she still lived in the same apartment decided to head on over right away. I stopped at the ATM on the way. Those were two things I knew about Elizabeth. If you didn't hurry she wouldn't be in one place long and it was always a good idea to have some cash. I hadn't seen her in two years but I was guessing that neither thing had changed.

Frequently I'm asked, often by women, about the appeal of the strip joint. They think it's skanky and cheap and it is all of that. But I need to answer on a couple of different levels. First we need to separate strippers from porn because while they are cousins they are quite distinct. But we will get more into that later. The main appeal at first is quite simple.

The Wal-Mart Chronicles . . .

When guys go out drinking we are trying to meet women, get drunk, and hook up. This rarely happens. As we get older it happens less and less. We also get wiser. More and more often we realize that at the end of the night we can just go see some naked women, talk to them, and get drunk without all of the silly embarrassment, harassment of the innocent women, and complicated use of various date rape drugs at the bar.

So that is what we do. We go see uncomplicated naked women. It's like Wal-Mart. You don't have to think about where to go or what to do. It's just the easiest and in the end the cheapest and the safest. So what if it degrades us all and the product enslaves a certain class of people.

The thing of it is, that some of us like it too much. We like talking to these girls more than we like talking to other women. We like their aura of damage. We can't differentiate between reality and fantasy because most of us are alcoholics or drug addicts, just like the girls, so all the lines blur.

It is an interesting thing, if you were to wander through a high end rehab and talk to the guys there, the alcoholics and the pill poppers and the clean cut crack smokers, fully 75% of them absolutely adore strippers and hookers. Just love them.

And it isn't a purely sexual thing although there is obviously a prurient aspect. There is the notion of another damaged soul, of someone as frightened as them, as lost as them, that might see them as strong. But also someone that quite literally never sees them in the light of day. It is a beautiful and a powerful thing to only be seen in the weak flourescents and colored floorlights of a strip club. For some reason they never had group sessions on this subject. As I said, I've had a few problems.

I got to Elizabeth's apartment and it didn't look too bad. It was clean with a lot of candles and beanbag chairs. All the windows were open and it was a cool spring night and it felt good. Her television was on and it appeared she still had cable which surprised me. I wanted to peek in the bedroom and see if her webcam was still up and going. To me it is the most bizarre and difficult to understand part of her life, which says more about me than about her. She hugged me and we sat on her couch.

I leaned back in one corner and Elizabeth took the other. She threw her slippered feet up in my lap and giggled. Flannel pajamas made her look even younger than her twenty-three years and with her hair back in a bandana she was to die for. Her skin was olive and she had a slightly Asian look, she claimed her mother was half Thai and her father was half Navajo but I never really believed the things she said. She may have just been Latina. Her weight was down and while it may have been unhealthy, it looked good. It carved angles and knowledge into the baby fat of her face. Her brown eyes seemed at least a little bit alive though she was obviously stoned. I asked her about the leg she said she had hurt.

Scooting towards my lap she showed me a large bruise on her thigh, something from an accident on the stage bar. Nothing that would need my attention. She giggled about not having shaved her legs. There were streaks of red from a couple of track marks behind her knee and I rubbed them gently with my finger but she didn't seem to notice.

Moving more on my lap she tried a stripper face and said she missed me and asked why I never called. She smelled of pot and jasmine and the funny thing was that I had called a couple of times and was always thankful she didn't call back.

She started to lean towards me, the way that strippers do, as if to kiss me, but not really, and I remembered what everything with Elizabeth had been like. The disconnect between mind and body. She could somehow look so warm and feel so cold.

"When was the last time you ate?" I asked her. She just stared and laughed.

I got up and looked through her cupboards. There was no food. None. The fridge was empty too. "Put on a coat" I said. "We're going to Wal-Mart." Elizabeth just smiled and clapped her hands. "I missed you so much."

It was about midnight when we got there. It wasn't my usual Wal-Mart. She lived across town and was nearer a different supercenter. Of course they are identical for the most part but this one was the mirror image of mine, the grocery store on the left instead of the right and the freezer section towards the back instead of the front. It was all very disorienting. A dyslexic shopping experience.

Elizabeth was bouncing off the walls. I was thinking she must have done a quick bump before we left. She was running down the aisles and sliding in her slippers. It had gotten pretty chilly before we went so she had on this furry vest over her pajama top and she wound a scarf around her head like a cancer patient or maybe Rhoda. She was quite the sight, gleeful and tiny.

That was another thing about strippers. They always seemed surprisingly little when I saw them away from their job. Down off the stage, not wearing heels, not standing over me preparing for a lapdance, it completely changed perspective.

She slid into a lady shopping with her three year old little boy and the lady pulled the kid away from her, as if she sensed something was wrong with Elizabeth, something missing, something empty. Elizabeth just hissed at her and ran away.

I caught up to her in Arts & Crafts, looking at thread and cross stitch patterns, talking about a present she had sewn for her mom in third grade. I watched her to make sure she didn't steal anything.

We picked up some bread and pasta and sandwich stuff that I doubted she would eat and some cereal that I knew she would and ended up in the freezer section staring at ice cream. I asked her what her favorite was.

"I don't have one. Not really. I never eat ice cream." she said.

A stoner, meth-head stripper that didn't eat ice cream seemed wrong to me but I wasn't sure why. I bought her some chocolate chip cookie dough and some heath bar crunch and some with reese's peanut butter cups in it. All of it was a whole new world to her.

Back at her apartment she sparked up a joint and ate a little ice cream, stunned at the taste. She watched tv and laughed a little and fell asleep around 3 am. The carton dripping in her small hand. She'd forgotten to tell me the real reason she had called.

It didn't matter. I knew. It was the 4th of the month, the 5th now. Her rent was due and she wanted money, some way or another. It is the nature of the transaction when you get right down to it. It can be nice and pleasant and at times even beautiful and lovely, but all of that dies when you tuck a blanket around her shoulders to keep her warm and leave her $400 on the counter. Another satisfied Wal-Mart shopper.

Peach Fest
(A Wal-Mart Chronicle)

The Wal-Mart Chronicles . . .

"If you wait for inspiration you'll be standing on the corner after the parade is a mile down the street."

Ben Nicholas

Things seemed a little different at Wal-Mart last night. Darkly festive I guess I would say. It was just past dusk and people were loitering in the lot. Hispanics mostly, sitting in the beds of trucks and leaning against tailgates.

Different age groups were in different areas with competing strains of music throbbing from car stereos. Slightly chunky teenage girls, I swear to god dressed in boxer shorts and bras, were leaning in windows in packs of three.

Low riding Japanese cars with illegal window tints and roof lights that looked like a marriage of California and red neck snaked through the parking lanes.

A couple of cop cars appeared to be in serious discussion, trying to decide if it was worth it to break any of this up. Some of the underwear clad teens were giggling and heading their way, chatting on cell phones and snapping each other's pictures. It was as if someone had declared some sort of discount retail giant Latin holiday.

In fact, it WAS a holiday of a sort. The town has been celebrating its yearly summer festival. It is a weeklong thing called the Peach Festival or Pear Festival or something like that ,and celebrates one of our favorite fruits that in reality are pretty scarce in this area. Mostly we have chickens here, and thus the recent influx of Mexicans as these chickens require catching, hanging, and cutting – all of which is hard and hot work. Historically, we aren't particularly fond of hard and hot work . Please see slavery for another good example. But I digress.

The Festival ends up with a Saturday parade that follows a 5K run that takes place in 100 degree heat every year. It is guaranteed to send at least ten people to the hospital and at one point had at least one death for three years in a row so they moved the start to 7 am. The parade this year featured a Festival Queen sweating through pancake makeup and trying to hide an early pregnancy. Her car was driven by her stepfather who is best known for running the best grow-op in town. A Little Miss Peach and a Little Mister Peach had been elected in all previous years but in the current climate of pedophilia and child abduction everybody had sort of lost their taste for it and the tradition had quietly been dropped. In stead they added a chubby girl and a black girl to round out the Queen's court.

The group behind the pageant queens was a gang of cancer survivors who all bought their weed from the family in the car just in front of them during their chemo treatments. Now they just keep on buying it out of politeness, and because it seems neighborly. Behind them was the high school band and they were all stoned on bud grown in an outbuilding that was built on the Festival Queen's barn. The tuba player was getting paranoid people who were noticing that he had knocked up his girlfriend the Festival Queen.

It was that kind of parade.

Interestingly, there were almost no Mexicans in the parade even though they are about 15-20% of the town now. Maybe it's because whatever peaches or pears that are harvested here are picked by them. Or maybe they just don't find fruit anything to celebrate.

In any case a separate holiday was declared it seems. A Wal-Mart holiday. A celebration of retail shopping. A shout out to the world that they lived in a land with 24 hour grocery, motor oil, and arts and crafts availability. They lived in America now and they would wear underwear as outergarments and make middle aged men feel guiltily turned on. This was their day too. Fuck the peaches.

Earl and Sports Mediocrity
(A Wal-Mart Chronicle)

The Wal-Mart Chronicles . . .

"O-o-h child, things are going to get easier.

O-o-h child, things will get brighter."

-The Five Stairsteps-

Wal-Mart scares me. It always has. Not the way K-Mart does. That's a whole 'nother thing. I don't want to talk about K-Mart here. That's too personal. The scars are too fresh. Let's stick with Wal-Mart.

Maybe it's the greeters that trouble me. I always seem to get the ones that look like they are about 7 days out from bypass surgery and maybe were on the pump a little too long. Their oxygen starved brains not quite hitting on all cylinders anymore. They lunge and stagger towards me like living Halloween characters bent on my happy destruction in a garden of discount retail delight.

People were happy in my Wal-Mart this morning. Too happy.

Didn't they know what was going on? How could they shop for food and yarn and motor oil and fungal creams and blenders and obesity books and aspirin and bullets at a time like this? Ok I can see the aspirin and bullets but the rest of it seemed completely out of line.

One of our local transvestites seemed tired from his long night. He was a sad transvestite to begin with. He often had a three day beard and his curly leg hair stuck out through his fishnet stockings. He tended to wobble on his bright red high heels. Quite frankly he seemed to have given up any sort of attempt at quality transvestitism.

"Earl" I greeted him.

"Doc" he said to me.

"Tough ballgame this weekend." I said.

"The Hogs suck, Doc. It's time to throw in the towel", Earl said and reached for some Cheez-its.

I asked him if he thought there was any kind of a curse on the Razorbacks. Maybe a Wal-Mart curse.

Earl looked at his big feet and said, "The only curse I can think of is the fact that they don't make these shoes in Men's size 12."

I just nodded and moved on. Nobody likes a pessimistic transvestite.

The Wal-Mart Chronicles . . .

I was gathering my things - detergent and light bulbs, deodorant and DVDs (Knocked Up dropped today) and watching faces. People kept whizzing by me on the little battery driven Rascals they give to the handicapped to move about the vastness of a Superstore. I began to notice that there were dozens and dozens of these things. I wondered if maybe I was in a "special needs" Wal-Mart but the shelves were regular height and the Depends undergarment section was not expanded so it seemed doubtful. I wondered if all of these people were as sad as me.

A 85 year old lady named Mabel rammed into my left leg with her scooter. She was an old ER acquaintance.

"Hey Doc," she said. "Wow the Hogs are bad." She paused and scratched the whiskers on her chin as if she had something else to tell me. "Oh yeah, my husband Duvall finally died last week."

"I'm sorry to hear that Mabel", I said.

"About which, the Hogs or Duvall? 'Cause you know Duvall was really, really old." Mabel just looked at me, wanting an answer.

"I guess I'm sorry about both, Mabel. I guess I'm sorry about both."

Lost in Automotive

(A Wal-Mart Chronicle)

The Wal-Mart Chronicles . . .

"It is important to tell good stories. You can tell stories even if they are not huge, epic and wonderful. You can still take responsibility for being a scribe for your tribe."

-Ajay Naidu-

Night falls a little harder on some of us than others. It isn't that it's gray or black or lonely or even depressing. For some of us it is all too alive and long and exciting and creative and sleepless and forever. The night doesn't have sharp edges like the day. Images and ideas blur into one another and somehow connect into bigger, more important seeming pictures.

The night to those of us that can't sleep can be the the tiny dots of light you see from a plane, scattered across the ground far below as you come in for a landing well after dark. Or the blinding headlights that pass as you drive cross-country on a lonely highway. The night contains the million little stories of people existing only with their internal dialogue, entertaining themselves with the voice that only they know, that comforts only them, that has it's own beautiful or haunting soundtrack.

For some reason my insomnia often leads me to Wal-Mart in the middle of the night. When I say often I mean a whole, whole bunch. Like I rotate the Wal-Marts out of embarassment and the various staffs STILL know me. This has been discussed at length with my therapist and she just says it's "weird" and tries to move on to a different subject. I'm okay with that.

So I was at Wal-Mart tonight, or this morning if you prefer, at around 1:30. The place had a certain gloom. Shopping carts were randomly arrayed throughout the parking lot as if there had been some sort of cart stampede just prior to my arrival. Three overweight guys in Wal-Mart golf shirts, black jeans and headphones trudged around the lot like sad modern day cowboys rounding up the strays.

Inside was livelier. Men were pushing around big rotating waxers. Stockboys with weak facial hair moved palletes of Tide, Cheer and Ramen noodles from place to place. They are all wearing ballcaps and headphones, enveloped in clouds of personal noise and rhythm. Lonely in a crowd. This is the sort of thing I think about in Wal-Mart. The sort of thing that the voice in my head that speaks only to me wants to talk about.

I hunted up and down various aisles for windhield wiper fluid. That was my mission for the evening, my retail quest.

Windex was easy enough to find but who knows if these things are the same or even similiar. They are both blue and smell like ammonia but you buy one in the kitchen cleaning section of the store and another in automotive. This might signal important differences in their underlying chemical structure. One seems fundamentally male and the other fundamentally female in the part of my brain that assigns sexual characteristics to inanimate objects (and sadly this is a rather substantial part of my brain).

So I continued to wander. Lost in "Automotive", as often happens to me. Sometimes I think that will be the title of my posthumous biography. "Lost in Automotive". It has a nice ring to it. I'm thinking Vince Vaughn will play me in the movie

Finally I ask a guy for help. He is setting up a DVD display and looks older than me but is very small in that sort of elfin way you see sometimes maybe as the manager of a rural high school basketball team.. He walks with a distinct limp and his nametag says "Rooney". He beckons me to follow and I realize that THIS is why I never ask for help - because people actually DO HELP and then I am forced to interact with them.

So I follow Rooney as he waddles down an aisle. I notice that he has cotton jammed in his left ear. It is soaked with something yellow and infected looking and some of it has dripped onto his shoulder. He smiles and shows me a HUUUUGE display stack of wiper fluid jugs. Rooney gives me a look that seems to indicate he is weary of dolts such as myself. I want to tell him that his head seems to be leaking some vital fluids but I stand there awkwardly as l the moment passes and my attention wanders to odder sights than cocky dwarves with ear infections.

There are single moms scattered about Wal-Mart late at night. There always are. They are there with their children because it is easier to shop at this hour. Or they just finished a swing shift. Or because they are embarrassed to use their food stamps at busier times of day. For whatever reason they are always here and so are their kids, yelping and screaming -the kids not the moms. The moms just look tired.

The Wal-Mart Chronicles . . .

One of these young mothers is in front of me in the checkout line. She is getting Tuna Helper and some underwear and cereal and chicken. Her hair is brown and slightly dirty and matted. She is probably 25 and might be pretty. I'm not sure. She has faint acne scars on her cheeks but her eyes are bright. She is wearing shorts despite the fact that it is 40 degrees outside and her legs are weird skinny, the knees knobby and bruised. Two boys that look about 5 or 6 are pounding each other at her feet, their faces smeared with dirt and their feet covered only by socks. Both have crewcuts and small scabs in their hairlines.

She smells strongly of smoke.

I quit smoking about 6 months ago but the smell is still divine to me. It is like $1000 perfume. Nectar of the gods. I honestly like the smell of ashtrays. I want to cuddle with one. I am not kidding.

I was sniffing the young lady in front of me in line. Even at 1:30 a.m. in Wal-Mart in Arkansas this is considered a social faux pas.

"What ARE you doin' ?" she asked.

"Um . . . you smell good. I mean, like cigarettes. Marlboro Lights I think. I just quit you see. I mean you really smell good." I responded with my usual quick wit.

"I smell like B.O." she said. "Is that you Doctor K.?" she asked, squinting at me.

Yikes. I don't work in my hometown much but I've spent a decent amount of time doing various STD and teen pregnancy clinics and I used to moonlight around here so this happens quite a bit (at Wal-Mart as well as on the dating scene). I should make it a rule not to sniff strangers.

I was leaving with my wiper fluid and a half-gallon of ice cream and the B.O. girl was waiting outside for me. Her maniacal children were stuffing their mouths with "super-sour" Spree, which are like Meth for the pre-teen set. "Did you want to bum a smoke Doc?" she asked.

She wasn't hitting on me. She was just one pathetic late night Wal-Mart shopper offering a life preserver to another pathetic late night Wal-Mart shopper. We are a tribe you see.

And I did want to bum a cigarette. I wanted to feel the smoke scald my lungs during the long inhale. I wanted to be warmed inside by the little friend that never leaves. Not even in the middle of the night.

"Just blow your smoke on me." I said. "Please."

And she did.

We stood there. A little awkwardly but not too much. We had nothing to talk about so she asked me about the Hogs hoop squad this year. I tried not to get started as people think me mentally ill when I get on a rant. She said she didn't know what to think about football season. That she missed DMac. That it was cool to see Kodi on TV at Auburn because her little sister knew him really well and he was a really nice kid.

I watched her boys as she talked. The taller one was popping more Sprees. He had red colored drool coming out of his mouth and he grinned like a fiend. He and his brother were running towards each other and butting heads like big horned rams and the "thwack" of their skulls hitting would echo across the parking lot.

The voice inside my head, the one that talks to only me, seemed pleased. "This is the fabric of your place." It said. "And this is your tribe."

Wal-Mart Sushi

(A Wal-Mart Chronicle)

The Wal-Mart Chronicles . . .

"Kids are like Slinkys. They get on your nerves but they are fun to push down the stairs every once in awhile."

Unattributed

I was babysitting my three nieces and a nephew. This would be bad enough by itself., but the nephew was five months old and seemed to be unamused by my dry wit and wry observations. Apparently sarcasm is wasted on neonates. This was leading to major issues including a crying jag that had gone on pert near 30 minutes and a series of rectal eruptions that I am sure registered on a seismograph somewhere and were overflowing the diaper that I had inexpertly applied. The air was alive with the scent of parenting and semi-digested breast milk.

To take my mind off of the task of wiping and cleaning I was discussing with my nieces the fact that the laws of physics didn't seem to apply to infants. For instance, we had here a child that weighed at most 15 pounds, yet in the last half hour he had produced at least that much weight in feces. This of course violated the law of conservation of mass, I explained. The girls nodded appreciatively (they are Newton fans all) while slowly backing away from me and moving towards the phone or perhaps the exit. I couldn't be sure. I knew I didn't like the look in their eyes. They were turning on me it seemed.

"Are you sure you know what you're doing Uncle Jay?" asked KiKi, the oldest and thus the bravest.

"You mean the diaper?" I giggled nervously, maybe like Michael Vick at the Westminster Dog show. "I'm cool. I'm all over this."

"NO!" shouted Boo, the middle girl, ten years old and suddenly fed up. "We mean ALL OF THIS. BABYSITTING. LIFE. You seem to be a little confused. Our ears hurt. Our noses are dripping. We're hungry."

I stared blankly into their pretty, shiny, yet strangely evil little faces. They were all nodding at me now. Showing me pity like you would the kid in class that doesn't read so good and only owns one shirt.

Maddog, the seven year old, said "Do you have any friends Uncle Jay? I mean real friends."

I wondered what she meant by "real". As opposed to plastic? electronic? or maybe just not very close? These kids were creeping me out. Maddog thought she was sooo cool these days because she could have sleepovers. I wanted to tell her that I had sleepovers with my friends too but it occurred to me that maybe this what what my sister meant when she referred to my "somewhat inappropriate conversations" with her children.

The fact of the matter was that the girls were right. I was adrift. A man without anchor or purpose. Unsure in movement. Lacking in conviction. It happens to me every summer. I lose myself sometime in late June. Sinking in the miasmic sea of the sportsless summer months.

Just a few days earlier I found myself cheering for a guy named Paddy to beat a dude named Sergio and it WASN'T an episode of Project Runway. That's exactly how bad things get in the summer.

The phone rang and interrupted our little stalemate. It was my brother Lawson, the father of the now smiling and babbling baby we call Fletch. (We call him Fletch because that's his name.) My brother was supposed to be babysitting with me. My sister and her husband and my parents and my sister-in-law were all out having a day and night on the town in Eureka Springs. They were doing those things that parents don't get to do because of their children - the things that I am free to do most every day but usually don't because quite frankly they are kind of a hassle at my age. It all seems so tiring these days.

But the childcare plan had been tweaked a bit. Lawson had been sent to Rogers on a quest for food, DVDs, candy and much ice cream. This seemed an excellent idea at the time and I recall we were even chanting BEN & JER - REYS! as he drove off. But problems soon cropped up.

The first of these has already been mentioned - I am not competent to care for children. The second was that Rogers was pretty far from the lakehouse where we were staying, much farther than we thought. The last problem was that my brother sucks at quests. He always gets sidetracked or confused or lost or arrested or loses his wallet. He is a Monty Python sketch waiting to happen.

My brother was talking too fast on the phone. I told him to slow down and repeat what he had just said because there was no way I had heard him right.

"Dude - the Wal-Mart here sells sushi."

"That's impossible!" I yelled. The girls looked up at me, startled.

"One would think." he said.

"Don't move" I said. "We'll be there as soon as we can."

"I'll be waiting. I'm having some Spicey Tuna and a California Roll." He paused, his mouth full of raw fish and rice. "Bring the spare set of keys too. I locked myself out of my car. I'd hurry if I were you. It looks like this ice cream is gonna melt pretty quick."

We were off.

People need a purpose in life. A focus. We had that now. I scooped up the bellowing micro-human and the girls followed like little soldiers with juice bottles and attitudes.

We hit our first snag only seconds later. It turns out car seats for babies are a HUGE pain in the butt. If the seven year old wasn't there we never would have figured that thing out. Luckily it faces backwards so I didn't have to look at his terrified and nauseated little face as we drove down the mountain roads.

Quickly the girls had Fletch laughing and spitting (and I couldn't be sure but it looked like they were putting lipstick on him) so we kicked the trip into high gear with some heavy tunes. We started off with "Ridin' Dirty" by Chamillionaire (a tribute to Fletch) then they made me listento Lupe Fiasco and I made them listen to Trick Daddy sing "I'm a Thug". We closed with some Neko Case and we were all happy and hoarse by the time we made it to Wal-Mart.

The sun had just gone down when we arrived. The huge building stood out like a retail cathedral in the gloaming. Inviting yet scary. Familiar but somehow changing into something different. My brother sat on the ground, leaning against his car. He was sipping a Mike's Hard Lemonade from a brown paper bag, smoking Camel filterless cigarettes, staring at the memory of orange and red in the western sky, listening to songs on his iPod from the musical "Wicked". On his lap was an open magazine with interior design ideas for the modern home and an empty carton of Ben & Jerry's Creme Brulee. My brother is an extremely confused man.

He waved as I unlatched his son and smiled as I handed the kid over, reveling in the aromas of fresh diarrhea and bubble gum lip gloss. Fletch drooled and smiled at his daddy.

I went inside the store and sure enough, right next to the deli a little guy was cutting and rolling up sushi. He didn't make it to order but just put it in a plastic container and set it out in front of him with a price tag. I took a picture with my phone and grabbed enough for all of us.

Outside we started to eat. The girls drank juice and watched a movie on my computer. We played some music softly from my car and waited for security to kick us out. They didn't. We had a little picnic right there on the asphalt.

The Wal-Mart Chronicles . . .

"Do you remember when Coke went plastic?" my brother asked.

Of course I did. Lawson had called me in the middle of the night my sophomore year in college. Growing up Coke always came in glass bottles. You could even get a six pack of quart bottles and then take them back when they were empty so that when you bought the next six pack you were basically just paying for the Coke itself - not the containers. We drank gallons of that stuff. It tasted different then. Somehow being in a glass is different than being in a can or in plastic. It started to change with the 2 liter bottles but they still had the 10 oz bottles and I think a 16oz size. Coke was the last to hang onto glass. But finally, one night, my brother noticed that there were no more glass bottles of Coke at the store. Coke had gone plastic, like everybody else.

It seemed like something changed that night. Maybe not. I think that was the same night Lawson said, "I just realized the three most important things in my life are sex, drugs, and rock & roll. I feel like such a cliche." Regardless, it was a transition of some kind. It marked something.

"I think Wal-Mart selling sushi is kind of like that." Lawson said.

I nodded, munching on a veggie roll with wasabi. Something old and comfortable had become something we didn't recognize - and it wasn't for the better. But that was time. It did stuff like that. This was just another benchmark.

Lawson smiled at his boy Fletch and Fletch made a strange noise. Maddog, Boo, and Kiki giggled and danced to a song on my stereo. And we all ate Wal-Mart sushi in the parking lot.

Spring Forth

(A Wal-Mart Chronicle)

The Wal-Mart Chronicles . . .

"A lap dance is so much better when the stripper is crying."
-The Bloodhound Gang-

Playoff basketball is trickling across my screen. I love the NBA with the "Amazing" and all but for me this is the denouement of the sports year. I watch them with music on in the background while I read a book or try to catch up on journals. Tonight, as I watch Denver and the Lakers, I have been most impressed by the intricate pattern of AI's cornrows and by the fact that Kyra Sedgewick seems to be turning into some sort of creepy reptile in front of a national television audience. It should also be mentioned that Kenny Smith's suit appear's to be made from the same material as my car seats.

I drift into melancholy and sober sadness as I watch playoff basketball. This always happens to me. I feel old and sad and lonely and I dread a summer of baseball and golf and sweat and getting into a boiling hot car with a steering wheel sticky to the touch. I want to be young and fit again like these guys are. I want to be able to run forever and bounce off wooden floors and feel the soft leather spin between my fingers. I want to be WEIGHTLESS. Instead I see the spring of my life slipping away once again.

Age and time bring with them some wisdom but they also bring some unwanted knowledge. I know what I am and what I will never be. I have become burdened by the weight of my limitations. They hold me in this chair watching mediocre basketball, listening to Beth Orten sing songs that are both hopeless and hopeful. It seems that adventure is gone from my life. It is pathetic that I look to sports for vicarious excitement but there you have it.

My mind has drifted as the games have ended. The Dave Matthews Band has given way to Radiohead and I am sketching imaginary houses on a pad, high ceilings and infinity pools, places I won't build but would be cool to live in, creating an alternate reality. Fruit flies buzz at my head and on the wall even though I am quite sure there is nary a fruit nor a veggie in the house. A stack of unread books teeters at an impossible angle near my chair next to a discarded wrapper from Wendy's. I am having "text sex" on my phone with a chunky woman from work who enjoys that sort of thing. I'm thinking about taking up smoking again. I've heard good things.

I step outside to dribble a basketball which is sure to anger someone because it is after 1 AM. The concrete is damp and the there are scattered puddles from an earlier storm. Clouds are backlit by the moon and move rapidly, clearing the

way for a spectacular night sky. The air is brisk and freshly washed and has that sense of recently discharged electricity. Trails of water come off the ball in a vertical plane as I toss it in the air and steady my stroke. The ball feels heavy but good as I launch a sad airball that is a foot to the right and over the goal. It bangs into my neighbor's car and sets off it's shreiking alarm.

"Go To Bed You Freakin' LOSER!!" someone yells out a window.

"And put some PANTS on for goodness sake!" they add in a not too neighborly tone.

I look down at my rather worn out boxer shorts and hang my head. I gather up my ball from a puddle of mud and plod inside.

I look around my sad hovel. Clothes are scattered in random piles and half finished sodas litter tabletops. Single shoes forlornly seek out their mates and for reasons I could never explain why their is a pile of feathers on the floor of the kitchen. I need to DO something. I need to GO somewhere. But where can I go at 1 o'clock in the morning?

I pull on some jeans and head for Wal-Mart.

Maybe I'll buy a movie, or an iPod. Maybe I'll get a really big tv. Maybe I'll buy a treadmill to symbolize my lifelong journey to nowhere. These are the kinds of possibilities that a Wal-Mart offers. Maybe I'll get a Blu-ray player since the format war is over. Maybe I'll buy some off brand golf balls that I will soon lose in the woods. Maybe I'll get some pajamas and slippers and decide to grow old gracefully. Maybe I'll get some yarn and teach myself to knit. Maybe I'll just lie on the floor and play with the yarn like a kitten. Maybe I'll get some double stuff Oreos and just eat the creamy centers. Maybe I'll get some Metamucil to improve my stool bulk. The world is my oyster at Wal-Mart.

In the end I do none of those things.

When I pull up in the parking lot a remarkably short guy that might be a midget except he is fat and has long arms has a shopping cart and is repeatedly trying to run over a guy that is curled up on the ground crying. A teenage girl with a hoodie, a bad complexion, and enough metal poking through her face to frighten pets and small children is screaming at the guy on the ground to "GET UP AND STOP BLUBBERIN' !"and to "PULL YOUR PANTS UP, YOUR CRACK IS SHOWIN'! ". Two cops are standing next to the whole mess looking like they might pepper spray the whole bunch but they can't stop laughing long enough to decide who they want to start with.

The greeter is in a wheelchair and might be 90 years old. She has rolled outside to watch the brawl and just gives me a wave as I walk by. She is grinning like a maniac and chattering on a cell phone. Thunder rolls in the background and for just a second I am convinced that this Wal-Mart is haunted.

So much for hauntings and adventure. I find myself in the pharmacy section staring at an UNBELIEVABLE assortment of cures for "digestive irregularities".

It's not that I have any stomach problems, but that I am looking for short cuts to weight loss and feel like perhaps variations on bulimia might be the way to go. There are numerous guys on late night tv and radio hawking bowel cleansers and "de-toxifiers" talking about 10-25 pounds of retained stool that coats our intestines like paste and is "toxifying" our bodies. One guy even says that at autopsy, John Waybe had 44 pounds of poop in his colon. (He fails to mention that this might have been due to either obstruction or severe constipation because of the massive amounts of narcotics required to control the horrible pain from his metastatic cancer but why let the truth get in the way of a sales pitch.) Of course I know this is all a bunch of silly lies. There is no paste and no plaque in our colons and intestines. I have seen WAY too many colons and intestines in my life. I have seen them thhrough scopes and during surgeries. I have seen them on Cat Scans and on MRIs. I have seen them clean and I have seen them dirty. I have seen them wide open on people's bellies after they have been shot or stabbed. I have even seen one with a vase inserted in it and one with several batteries uncomfortably nested. I have even seen a picture of one with an unopened umbrella wedged inside. I know me some intestines. One thing I have NEVER seen is a "plaque" or a "paste". Intestines and colons are universally shiny, squishy, and very slimy on the inside with some blood, poop, pus, polyps, and tumors mixed in. No paste. No plaque. Lots of yuk.

But . . . the thing is that the guy on late night television with the sickly yellow/green complexion telling me my body is filled with toxins may have a tiny point. I MIGHT be able to lose 10-20 pounds by inducing 2 weeks or so of rampant diarrhea. Wrestlers, ballerinas, and high school cheerleaders in Texas have been doing this for years. It strikes me as an excellent idea.

I sense a presence next to me. A presence with a voice. It smells like peach Jolly Ranchers (The presence not the voice). I feel I am about to be embarrassed.

"This looks like a good section for you Jay. You've always been completely full of . . ." the voice starts before I cut it off. It is a familiar, female voice. Pleasant but a little hoarse, like she has a permanent sinus infection.

"Hey now. Be nice or I'll get THAT." I point to the Fleets Enema. "And wash out the bug that's been living up your . . ." This time she cuts me off.

"Okay, okay" Lizzie says. " I'll try to be friendly."

I turn to look at her. I have to look down because she is tiny and I am not. She is maybe 4'11" and I'm about 6'6". People always ask me why I like short women and I don't know what to say. It isn't like I have been picky all these years. Short women like ME. To them my size gives the illusion of strength. Once they get to know me they find out I don't have any but it works for a while. You play the cards you're dealt.

Lizzie looks good. She has gotten old like me. She would be 40 now too, but when you see someone your own age the years don't really count. Her face has lines and creases now and her hair is thinner and cut shorter and maybe she looks like a mom but her nose is still kind of red and she is still neat and pretty and has big brown eyes and nice white teeth with one crooked one on the bottom. I haven't seen her for about 8 years, since she got married. She married the next guy she went out with after me. That seems to happen a lot. Apparently something about me is so horrifying that ANYONE seems perfect after dating me. I feel like I provide a service in that way.

"I got divorced", Lizzie says without expresion. We were now shopping together and she had just selected several boxes of condoms and was now picking through a few choices of thong underwear.

"I kinda guessed", I said.

I was now in a bit of a quandry. It is impossible to watch a woman buy condoms without mentally picturing her having sex, especially when you have ACTUALLY had sex with her. And it's very difficult to carry on an intelligent conversation with a woman while you are imagining having sex with her. (This, in fact, is one of the reasons men seem so stupid most of the time.)

"You want to watch a movie? I was about to buy "Juno"." I asked her out of the blue.

"Is that your totally uncool way of asking me for a booty call?" Lizzie raised an eyebrow when she said it. I wasn't sure if I detected a smile.

"Well, I was sort of looking for some adventure tonight." I tried to explain.

"Adventure? At Wal-Mart?" She snorted. "Sex with you? Adventure?" She started laughing uncontrollably and wouldn't stop. I laughed with her for a minute but after a while it started to hurt my feelings. She just kept laughing.

"I think I'm gonna wet myself" she said. And I was concerned that she might. She sat down on the floor in the socks section and just kept laughing, wiping tears from her eyes.

"I'm not entirely sure I like your attitude young lady" I said. Lizzie tried to respond but she couldn't talk. She just held up her hand and kept laughing, tears and snot streaming down her mean little face.

I thought back to our time together which, truth be told was pretty unremarkable. My biggest selling point is that I am amusing and can make people laugh. That only goes so far. I thought about our love life and our time in bed. I thought about the noises she made, the weird grunts that seemed to come from some place outside of her and that strange urgency she had when she wanted me to pull her hair or maybe talk dirty. I thought about how disassociated from all of that I always felt, like I was watching an absurd and kind of funny movie of my own life. I remembered how she would get a little smile of happiness and that as soon as I was finished I would always say something sorta funny like "Well that was interesting" or "I gotta get in shape" or maybe "Ouch I think I pulled something" because I was humiliated that someone had just seen my sex face and because I wanted to change the mood from "let's cuddle" to "I'm gonna get a sandwich".

"So you didn't enjoy any of that, huh?" I asked. I asked because I knew that she did at least a bit. That she was hurt when we broke up.

Lizzie was still laughing but she could talk now. "Jay you were fun and all but I'm not sure I'd call it an adventure. I loved the way you made me laugh. I even kind of liked those creepy things you would say after sex. It was like you were reminding me that sex with you was supposed to be a comedic experience."

"Uhhhhhhhhh"

"Sure Jay, let's watch "Juno". I could use a good laugh."

The greeter was snoring in her wheelchair as we left and the parking lot was empty. The cops were gone and the fight was over and it had started to rain. It wasn't storming, the rain was just dripping from the sky reminding us it was there, splashing my face and making little puddle.

DOG'S WORLD

"I loathe people that keep dogs. They are cowards that haven't got the guts to bite people themselves."

August Strindberg

"Quit saying prison Sammy. This isn't prison. This is jail. Prison is a place you go if you get convicted of somethin'. Do you grasp the distinction Sammy?" The mocha colored prostitute seated next to me in this crowded courthouse is peering at me. Hoping for some simple sign of understanding.

I nod my head. "Yes Candy, I understand. And stop calling me Sammy." This last is with emphasis. My name is not Sammy. It is Jordan Samuel Day. The third actually. I hate to be pretentious but I've never been a Sammy. Jordan is just fine thank you. Or Tres, like the spanish for three, which is what the few friends I have tend to call me. Or Jay, which is what my mom calls me on days that she sits on her recliner in a valium induced haze. But never Sammy. Sammy is a dog's name. It's my dog's name. And its that fucking dog that got me here in the first place.

"I don't like none of those names Sammy. They sound like you're putting on airs." Candy is whispering in my ear and trying to cross her legs in a ladylike fashion, a task made difficult by the spandex pants riding up her crotch and ass. Her breath smells like rotting wine. "And prison is no place to start getting uppity."

"Jail", I say with my mouth half covered and my face buried in my stubby fingers.

"Right you are Sammy. Learnin'. That's all I can ask of you. That's all that anyone can ask of you."

I eye her through my fingers. She is difficult to describe. She looks both fifteen and forty. Her skin is the icteric yellow of the cirrhotic or perhaps, the overly fanatical vegan. Her lips are thin and her lipstick just slightly smudged, like she's just been caught giving her boyfriend a nobber in the backseat. She is wearing a red shoulder length wig that needs a good brushing. Her eyes flit about, alive and hungry, swallowing everything that stirs around her. A strand of dark brown hair has escaped her wig and is dangling near her left ear, practically inviting me to pull it. She has lumpy breasts that are sagging prematurely and I imagine her nipples as huge and having no true end. Smoker's wrinkles around her mouth somehow seem cute and almost attractive. It is impossible to look at that mouth without thinking of where it has been, and where it will go. If it wasn't so early and I wasn't so hungover, I might have been a bit turned on.

"You still haven't tole me what they got you for Sammy. Solicitin' ?"

"No."

"You didn't strike me the type. Come on. You tell me yours, I'll tell you mine."

"I know yours." I immediately regretted it. She looked hurt and childlike again. Stung by disapproval.

I wonder what I look like to people walking by. I wonder what I look like to this young lady of the evening, and she is indeed young I have decided. We are sitting together on a bench in a holding area of the courthouse, one floor down from the cells we recently occupied. We had been together for two hours waiting to be picked up by the people who bailed us out. It was almost noon on a Saturday and the drunks that had made my cell a squishy vomitorium had all gone home. It was just me and six hookers. The desk Sargent wanted to move me away from them, concerned I suppose that I would become aroused and resume my sexual crimes of the night before. But my arresting officer said I was "harmless" and should be left alone. For some reason this hurt my feelings.

I decide to try to look menacing so I furrow my brow and clear my throat a lot. Candy laughs at me, looking me up and down. I am wearing loafers and white athletic socks with a pair of khaki shorts and a pajama top. Its tough to look menacing in that outfit. My legs are frighteningly pale and for some reason seem to be losing their hair in spots, like I have mange or something. My face is round and lost all its definition about thirty pounds ago. I badly need a shave. My head is bald save grayish strands that sprout owllike from above my ears. Thickish lenses perch on my huge forehead in what I call the professor position but at this moment I realize a more appropriate name would be the kiddie - porn mogul position. I am thirty eight years old and this is my first arrest. I wonder if anybody here knows I'm a doctor.

"I'm charged with assault, sexual battery, drunk and disorderly, public intox, public nuisance, possession of a controlled substance, cruelty to animals, and bestiality."

"Cool." Candy is nonplussed. She eyes me. Reappraising in light of my impressive list of charges. "You don't seem that drunk though."

"I'm starting to sober up. It was all that damn dog's fault." Candy can't suppress a little smile at this. Imagining, I suppose, the frumpy doctor with pants around his ankles coupling with a canine.

"I would think that bestiality would presuppose cruelty to animals. Sort of by definition. Unless of course they think the animal at times consents. I guess then you could commit the crime of having sex with the animal without necessarily being cruel." Candy looks thoughtful as she says this. As if such distinctions have great bearing in a career such as hers.

I like this woman. I like the way she thinks. She sees things like bestiality more clearly than the rest of us. If she would have been there none of this would have happened. She would have made everybody understand.

"They just tacked on the bestiality thing to be mean.`' I say. "A complete fabrication."

"I assumed as much. I was just thinkin' in terms of semantics. Inaccurate language offends me."

I stared at her. Excited by her knowledge. "They do?" I ask.

"Do what?"

"Tack on bestiality charges just to be mean?"

"Sure. If they think you're some kind of sicko they add it to the arrest record. Sort of as a red flag for next time."

I am momentarily comforted by this, then rethink. "So they think I'm a sicko?"

Candy gives me a motherly look. Scoots next to me. Her surprisingly long arm reaches around my round shoulders. I can see a decent nest of nappy hair under the arm. She smells of sweat and an unidentifiable funk. She kisses me lightly on the ear. "We're all sickos Sammy. If it were against the law we'd all be in prison."

"We are in prison."

"No we're not Sammy, we're in jail."

I rest my smooth head on her bare and aromatic shoulder. Finding warmth, comfort, and motherly affection in the arms of a teenage whore. The only one who can understand my story.

"The other day a dog peed on me. A bad sign."

H. L. Mencken

My story, dear Candy, is one of depth and distinction. It is about sexuality, reproduction, domestic violence, personal boundaries, alcoholism, drug abuse, animal husbandry, evil neighbors, questionable yard care, useless girlfriends, fruitless jobs, and big dogs. Really big dogs. Or maybe its just the story of a bad day.

The really big dog in question is Sammy, my Great Dane. Sammy is a her, short for Samantha and please don't start in on me about giving dogs people names. Its none of your goddam business.

I know I seem touchy on the subject but it just seems I spend an inordinate amount of time defending my actions. All of my actions are purely rational. People would understand all of them if they were just there. Well, not understand, but at least see that I am an entirely harmless individual. But they never are. Present I mean. My entire life is taken out of context. I am a badly misunderstood first time felon.

So I have this really big dog. Huge. Gigantic. Words fail me. If I'd had any sense at all I would have simply named her Really Big Dog and gotten it over with. All the startled looks of my invited guests, the shrieks of horror, their slobber drenched clothes, it all could have been avoided.

But you had to be there. She was so little when I brought her home. Those floppy puppy feet and that horse like head. I suppose I should have known she would grow, that in fact such an occurrence was so likely as to be considered unavoidable save some radical hormonal therapy. That Sammy would be an inadequate name to encompass all the dog she would soon become. I should have known everything. As ususal I knew nothing. But see, just yesterday the local noon news was showcasing a humane society puppy and the stiff and shiny anchorwoman reminded us all that the dog would grow quite a bit so be sure you have enough room for him. So apparently I'm not the only person around unable to forecast a sunrise on the following day. It was a bad call but made with a good heart while very drunk and watching an episode of Bewitched (First Darren, pre - Tabatha)

So my little puppy grew into a 185 pound horse sized behemoth as clumsy as she is large. And she thinks she's a cat. I guess that's my fault. I thought she would be lonely when I was at work so I got a kitty as a playmate. The cat remains unnamed, as all cats should. I refer to him alternately as The Cat, The Fucking Cat, and Useless Neutered and Declawed Bastard. He has yet to purr.

As far as getting along with Sammy, The Cat worked out well. Too well. The Fucking Cat quickly established himself as the brains of the operation with Sammy serving as his dimwitted sidekick, a brainless enforcer doing the bidding of the smart but tiny sociopathic gang leader. Sammy would pull clothes off their hangers and push them into a pile where The Cat would curl up and sleep, eventually leaving a circle of hair and often a urine stain behind. Sammy would knock over tables and chairs and once even broke my tv. All this Sammy would do utterly without malice. She was just hanging out with the wrong crowd. I tried to coax The Fucking Cat to stay in line by banning him from the house for one night but when I woke up my loafers were filled with piss and there was a snot smear on the sliding glass window where Sammy had pushed it open to let his boss in during the night. I started to yell at my dog but I didn't have the heart. I just watched her sit all folded up on the kitchen table, giving herself a bath by licking her paws then rubbing her head.

My life is dominated by these pets. I keep a house with a large yard so they can have room. I have a cleaning lady come in three times a week to pick up after them. I tolerate stench and disorder. All in the name of having a little company. In the name of having someone or something to yell at. A moving target at which to throw the breakable objects of my choice.

Which I guess brings us to me. I am essentially an unattractive middle aged man whose childless marriage has long since ended, mercifully. I am a former cardiologist who lost one too many malpractice cases and had a seeming inability to hide his frequent drunkenness and now works in a doc-in-a-box patting knees and handing out blood pressure meds and decongestants. Its not challenging but neither is it time consuming. I work ten hours a day, four days a week. I do not maintain hospital patients and I never take call. For this I am obscenely compensated.

My home is bachelor perfect save The Fucking Cat. It is spacious with two levels and a vaulted living room with a twenty foot ceiling. I have two big screen tvs, a well stocked bar featuring various single malts, and a room solely dedicated to smoking, drinking, and sporting events. The yard is a jungle and is ignored out of principle, not out of slovenliness. It is rumored in the neighborhood that several children have wandered into the dense foliage that is my front yard and were never heard from again. I never deny these rumors. In fact I started them.

I am considered a regular at three separate bars. I golf at least once a week at a lovely country club, membership to which was obtained during my salad days as a cardiologist. I don't have a bevy of buxom babes but I do have a regular thing with a superbly witty and only partially mentally unbalanced woman. I have no close friends but many acquaintances. I walk around naked in my house a lot and urinate in the sink whenever I want.

At this point readers will have divided themselves into two camps regarding my life. Those that think its perfect and those who see a desperately lonely man with squandered talents and a disdain for the community. An egomaniacal overgrown child unwilling to take responsibility for anything more important than a big dog and an evil cat. I tend to agree with both groups.

The one thing I absolutely lack is a conversation partner. By partner I mean someone willing to sit quietly and listen while I rant and rave in an incoherent drunken monologue. I mean someone who lets me howl at the top of my lungs and still acts interested. I mean someone who forces me to verbalize thoughts as I sit entranced in front of the flickering television, thus making my ideas more coherent and more real. It is here that the pets come in.

They are my sounding board, my rapt audience. As I may or may not have said, I am a drunk, but not much of a drinker. I get sloshed after 4 - 5 beers, 3 glasses of wine, or 2 stiff drinks. I do this frequently. When I do I become extremely verbal, and I feel really silly if nobody at all gets to hear me. So I yell things at the animals. Intellectual nuggets like about how freaked out I am by religious television preachers with unbelievably bad hair and how I wonder if God is very happy about his messengers looking like dorks. Or about my theory that John Grisham and Garth Brooks are actually the same person and though they are likely nice and decent people that isn't the point. Their prodigious publication of shallow and vapid works with the depth and aftertaste of cotton candy, is slowly eroding our ideas of true quality, a true sense of beauty, and they make this whole world just a little less interesting, a little less vital. And isn't that what the devil would do, slowly lower us into mediocrity, prevent us from developing our potential.

So I guess my theory is that not only are Brooks and Grisham the same person. They are Satan. My pets hear all this.

I also throw things at them. Things like pillows or wads of paper. The occasional scotch tumbler smashes dangerously close to their heads. They scowl and whine and cower but pretty much couldn't care less. I share insights into Stallone's career, Jackie Bisset's numerous assets and failure to appear in even one good movie her entire career, questioning aloud whether Josie Bisset from Melrose Place might possibly be kin, the perkiness of a new tv anchorwoman, neatly outfitted, overly made up, and ringless, of course. I spew hateful things at television politicos and the moronic masses that are allowed entrance to my home through a thick black cable. I tend to do all this in a rather loud voice. I think maybe my neighbors noticed.

"Neighbors are rats without tails. In other words, very much like the French."

Travis Buzzard

My neighbors are also a character in this minor tale. I don't know if other people have the same problems with their neighbors that I do. I suspect it exists on some level for everyone. Mine has just gotten out of hand. They hate me. They despise me in myriad ways. They whisper about me in small groups. Plot my demise over fence tops. They hate me because I'm unattractive and just a tad idiosyncratic. They hate me because I have no children. They hate me because they hear loud obscenities emanating from my house. They hate me because my yard is an eyesore and lowers the values of surrounding homes. They hate me because my dog is so big she is seen as a very real threat to their children. They hate me because said dog once ate three cute little bunnies that were pets of the eight year old girl next door.

I hate them back. I hate them because they are skulking, sniveling, clean scrubbed young professionals whose only concerns seem to be cars, clothes, property values, and fertility. Mostly the fertility. All the women are pregnant, pushing a stroller, nagging their man to switch to boxers, or crying themselves to sleep at night regretting that nasty chlamydial infection that has left their tubes scarred and twisted. All feel threatened by me and my Really Big Dog. They scurry to the other side of the street when me and Sammy barrel down the road at them. They have little poodles and schitzus. I dream of getting a boa constrictor and raising it to a length of twenty feet then setting it free in the neighborhood to devour their pets and their young.

People always think it is strange that when a serial killer is caught all his neighbors seem to say he was such a good person. Such a good neighbor. It should not be a surprise. This is because psychopaths and sociopaths are exceptionally good neighbors. They are quiet. They keep to themselves. They don't gossip. And they are very, very, very concerned about their yards. Burying bodies and dining on the flesh of young Asian boys isn't nearly as offensive as having a Really Big Dog and some weeds. Hell, I'd prefer card carrying members of ManBLA (Man - Boy Love Association) or those guys in Sausalito that get off on having prepubescent children shit on them for neighbors than the homogenous bunch of white bread pussies I'm surrounded by. Like I said, I hate them, and they hate me.

I suppose it was all this hate that started me down the road to my demise, but I can't quite be sure. Seeing all of that fertility and overly earnest reproduction pushed me over the edge. I decided I wanted to breed Really Big Dog. Not that I wanted more huge mammals ranging around my house, it was just another way to terrorize, and compete with, my neighbors.

You'd think that breeding dogs would be a pretty simple thing. And it probably is for most people. Unfortunately I'm not most people. All I knew was that I had to find another Great Dane to fornicate with my darling Sammy. So I placed a personal ad, and included my home phone number. At this point I realized that the vast majority of people reading and responding to personal ads were extremely disturbed and frightening people. Serious males for the most part. They spoke of "ejaculatory volume" and "sperm motility". It was apparent that these men felt their dogs to be quite strong in these areas. Several women called thinking that my ad was intended to debase women by referring to them as bitches and breeders and as they enjoyed being debased they wanted to get together.

I finally settled on a teenage kid that wanted half the pups for himself. I told him to bring a pint of bourbon and he just laughed and said "For you or the bitch?" It took a minute before I got it.

Jason Callin arrived one week later. Really Big Dog had entered estrus, at least I thought she had, taking her rectal temperature to predict ovulation turned out to be a dangerous and mucous filled experience so I just eyeballed it instead, and the rendevous was set. Jason pulled up at my quiet suburban house on a Friday night, the eve before this fateful morn on which I relate my little tale. His chariot was a beat up red Chevy pickup with an impressive beast perched in the bed, silhouetted against the fading fall light. I could see my neighbors, peering out from behind their paisley curtains, preparing for a night of socializing and high school football, envisioning the crazed and balding doctor slowly amassing an invasion force of large canines. Not so sure they wanted to leave little Dylan or Coby with the sitter tonight.

Jason climbed out of his jacked up truck like he was hopping off a stagecoach. He looked like your average AA high school defensive end who had just recently started fucking his long time girlfriend. Big, steroid bloated, poorly dressed, swaggering, and a shitty shave. He let fly with a glob of tobacco juice that arced gracefully before splattering across my ice cream colored sidewalk. "So where's the bitch?" He spit again, this time on my driveway.

I paused for a second, unable to get my head around this particular usage of the noun. Eventually I found my voice. "Inside on the recliner. Let's just take this fella 'round back. What's his name?"

"Shakespeare". He must have noticed that I was slightly taken aback because he was quick to explain. "Ya see, in English we had ta read this poem, sonnet I mean, 'bout this woman who's kind of a dog. You know, 'shall I compare thee to a summer's day' and all that. My girlfriend Trish thought it was really cool, so she made me name the dog Shakespeare. Not that Trish is a dog or nothin'. She just thought it was a cool poem, you know. Like a nice sentiment."

I just nodded for a second and he kept talking. "'Cause like the end of the poem is like that even if she wasn't beautiful she'll live forever because he wrote about her in the poem. Trish thinks stuff like that is cool. So she wanted me to name the dog after the poem like, so that our feelings might outlive us."

More nodding from me as we lead the beast around to the back yard. He was a well behaved animal but I must admit his maleness swinging freely beneath him was somewhat intimidating.

We set Shakespeare free in the backyard as dusk closed in. "You bring that bourbon like I asked Jason?"

He got kind of an aw shucks sheepish look about him. "Ah didn't have time to go by the liquor store so I jist grabbed a bottle of Daddy's scotch."

As we passed through my sliding glass door Jason pulled a fifth of 18 year old Macallan from his coat. Daddy will be pissed. Sammy reluctantly rose from the recliner and headed out to the backyard. I pulled a couple of chairs up to the window and grabbed a couple of tumblers. I have a fold up bar that flips down over the glass door and I leaned back and put my feet up on it. Jason did the same. Both of us staring quietly out at the backyard.

I poured him two fingers and handed him a Macanudo. He just looked at the drink for a second, confused. "No ice or nothin'?"

"Not with this stuff Jason. Just puff and sip." He did and seemed to be enjoying himself, up to his eyeballs with the self satisfaction of youth. We polished off a couple of glasses and things were getting warmer inside of me, the way they always do when I drink. Its as if just the smell of booze awakens the dormant animal within me, shaking off the cobwebs of consciousness and seeing the world fresh and new, ready to be demolished. The dogs seemed to be avoiding each other.

"You realize that Shakespeare will die before you do."

“What’s that?” Jason’s response was half choked as he dried to gulp his drink.

“Your dog,” I repeated. “He’s gonna die before you do.”

“Yeah, I know.” He looked almost wistful though I doubted him capable of such a subtle emotion. More likely his look was caused by reflux. The two are often confused.

“What I mean is that naming your dog Shakespeare won’t make your love outlive you since the dog will be dead.”

“Well, that’d be true except Trish and me are gonna break up after this year.” He stated this calmly as a simple matter of fact as he absently scratched himself in several hard to reach places.

“Why would that be?” Generally I couldn’t care less about other peoples lives but I have a very real weakness for other people’s personal sadness. I find the misery of others quite uplifting.

“‘Cause she’s moving to Boston to go to college. I can’t see myself following her up there.” I just drank and let him go on. “You know, I was just thinkin’, about how to breed dogs all you have to do is put them in the same room and sooner or later they’ll start havin’ sex. But with people its just the opposite. When we get put together instead of looking for what we have in common and going at it happily like dogs we search out and find the differences that make it impossible to get along. Like with me and Trish. Its like we were born on separate planets. She can’t imagine life without college and she can’t picture herself with anythin’ less than a professional job. I can’t picture myself with a job that doesn’t require a name tag or force me to take a shower when I’m done. Like we were born apart and that distance is always there. Never closed, never changing. Just a big empty space.”

I lifted my glass to his and toasted his precocious fatalism. A kindred spirit in negativity and unexamined cynicism. I wanted to tell him that we are more like the dogs than he thinks. That all relationships are like the one night together in the yard, a natural event followed by returning to our lives and completely forgetting those that we left behind. Tell him that this is the only way to survive because if we hung on to all of the past, to all of the things and people now lost to us, we would be catatonic with grief.

“You’re a doctor, right?” Jason asked, pie - eyed drunk and staring at the world through the bottom of his tumbler, the images far off and contorted.

“Yeah” I responded with my usual line to avoid curbside consults. “But I’m not a good one.”

"Doesn't matter. I just want to ask you somethin'." He paused and seemed to roll his tongue around his mouth, as if exploring for the first times its ridges, tastes and contours. He quickly snapped out of it and went on. "Trish, about a month ago, had this rash on her, well, on her pussy if you'll excuse my language. It looked like a group of fever blisters and she said it hurt like hell. But then it went away so I didn't think about it anymore. But now I've got it so it started me wondering. Whatcha think doc?"

"Herpes" I said without looking at him.

"What?"

"You and Trish have herpes."

"Mother fucker. That fucking bitch pardon my language again." He paused as we both finished our drinks and then he smiled. "I guess that's reason number two not to follow her to Boston."

"All God's children are not beautiful. Most of God's children are , in fact, barely presentable."

Fran Lebowitz

Jason informed me that sometimes these things take a couple of days. He seemed a knowledgeable source about such things so we decided to let the dogs stay outside together overnight. Jason drunkenly clambered into his pick - up and peeled out. Feeling suddenly alone, I went inside to watch tv, feeling the judgmental eyes of my neighbors boring into my round shoulders.

Watching television is perhaps my greatest pleasure and my set is rarely off. Unfortunately, by this time, I was quite drunk and inclined to yell a bit. I yelled at Noah Wyle on an E. R. rerun, because of the ease with which he placed a central line. I screamed again at the young punk, wondering aloud when he was going to rotate to another service. I bitched about the presentation of nurses as all - knowing and extremely competent, of EMTs as quick thinking and always at the ready with a concise summation of the situation, of residents who constantly shock asystole, a cardiac rhythm that does not respond to defibrillation.

It just wasn't working. I felt uncomfortable and out of sorts. My only watching partner was The Fucking Cat and cats are notoriously bad listeners. He would occasionally glance my way, blink slowly, then return to his fourteenth nap of the day. I hurled my scotch glass over his head, smashing it and leaving a stain on the wall. He didn't flinch. Just glanced back at me. Then asleep again. Regarding me as a crude and boorish person, barely tolerated by his feline highness.

I returned to my window perch and observed the mastodons of the suburbs. Sammy was extremely tense and agitated, hopping around and howling. Shakespeare would need a cold shower. I sipped my drink, bourbon now, and puffed on my cigar. Feeling docile and slightly horny. Wondering if Maryanne, my youngish, divorced, sometimes companion, would make an appearance tonight. It was here that I made my second fateful decision.

Why not get Sammy drunk? It only seemed fair. It was the only way I had ever gotten a woman in bed. Why should Shakespeare have to operate without the advantages the rest of the male sex take for granted? Just a little social lubrication to push things along.

So I called my Really Big Dog inside. She'd never been so happy to see me, standing to her full height, placing her paws on my shoulders, licking my face. I filled her bowl with a bottle of Heineken and tossed in some ground beef to get her started. I think I read somewhere that dogs don't like alcohol. My dog did. She loved it. She slopped up the beer and the burger in a few laps of the tongue. I poured her another, then finally a third.

Sammy belched and came to sit by me on the couch, curling up in imitation of her cat counterpart and panting foul beer breath in my face. "Don't get too comfortable hun. You still have a long night in front of you."

I led her by the collar to the sliding glass door. Shakespeare was standing at the window looking anxious and rather frightful. His giant head and tongue startled me and I guess they scared Sammy too because she yelped and retreated to the back of the room.

Frustrated, drunk, and more than a little irritated I closed the curtains and decided to get serious. I filled Sammy's bowl with half a bottle of Beefeater gin, half as much Schweppes, and added half a lemon. Thinking that if Shakespeare couldn't get her with a gin and tonic then he just wasn't trying.

Sammy refused to come out of her corner. She looked scared and confused, like a sixteen year old boy on a date with Madonna. I toted the world's largest gin and tonic to the center of the room and placed it on the floor. I knelt beside it and called my Really Big Dog over. She just growled and held her ground. So I placed my head in the bowl and began lapping up the liquid, trying to show Sammy how it was done. Not too bad actually, a little warm but otherwise quite refreshing.

My jealous dog came over to the bowl and tried to nudge me out of the way. At this point I was enjoying the game and continued to butt her head and get in a few drinks myself. Sammy would push me away and slop large gulps down her gullet. As we played and drank the front door opened. My sometime lover and sort of girlfriend, Maryanne, stepped into the room and stared down at us. Sammy and I, both kneeling and facing the door, looked up from our cocktail guiltily.

"They talk of my drinking but never my thirst."

Scottish Proverb

"Love is the delightful interval between meeting a beautiful girl and discovering she looks like a haddock."

John Barrymore

My dear Maryanne, who I once found quite attractive, is definitely approaching a fish - like appearance. I suppose this could be the cause of my great thirst.

Maryanne is a twenty - nine year old woman who has been my companion for over a year. Her short brown hair is whispish and rarely combed. Her skin is perfect and has never seen any make - up. She has large brown eyes that are lively and expressive. She is always dressed in flannel shirts, jeans, and Keds. Her figure is fading a bit but she looks a lot better than I do.

I met her, of course, at a bar, and have been seeing her three or four times a week ever since. She is a raving alcoholic, which suits me fine. She writes a column for a local alternative newspaper. She is quite funny but has a difficult time separating fact from rumor. Her politics lie just to the left of Mao Zedong. We are a good couple only in the sense that we both love to yell at the tv, me at entertainment, her at news and information.

She used to tell me about her failed marriage and her cheating husband. I took these rantings at face value. Now I find myself sympathizing with the poor sap. Her mood swings are rapid and vicious. Her insults at times sting. Her sensibilities are rigid and often juvenile. Her understanding of subtlety and nuance is nonexistent. Her personal hygiene has become increasingly dubious. She hasn't shaved her legs since last christmas.

"I don't even want to ask." She closed the door and dropped her purse on the couch.

"Hi honey. Just havin' a drink with my dog." I offered, looking appropriately embarrassed .

"Jesus Christ, is that gin?" Sammy belched loudly as she lapped up the last of the liquid.

"Uh - huh." I crawled over to the couch where she was sitting and sat down at her feet, leaning against the rough hair on her legs. She gently scratched the few remaining hairs on the back of my head.

I wanted to explain but my tongue was thick and my thoughts jumbled. "I jist wanted to breed ol' Sammy there. You know, make puppies." Sammy belched again.

"I wasn't aware that human and canine DNA were compatible." She rose and went to the bar and poured herself a scotch, threw it back, then poured herself another. I chose to remain slumped at the foot of the couch.

"Not with me hun, with Shakespeare." I pointed out to the backyard.

"Who the hell is Shakespeare?"

"Jason's dog.?

"Who's Jason?"

"The kid with the pick - up and the herpetic girlfriend."

"What are you talking about Jay?"

"I will not be grilled like a common criminal. Fix me a drink woman."

"You want it in a glass or a bowl?" She kicked me in the shin as she moved again to the bar. A little too hard if you ask me. Her bartending was interrupted by a thud against the sliding glass door. She screamed.

"What the fuck was that?"

"Shakespeare."

Maryanne opened the curtains and screamed again. Shakespeare's figure covered the entire glass. His mouth wide open as he stood on his hind legs. Maryanne kept screaming. The Cat rose from his position on the floor and went upstairs, showing clear disdain for us all.

"Shut the fuck up, Maryanne. Its just a dog." I screamed it to be heard over her wails.

"He's the ugliest beast I've ever seen." She drained her glass and poured herself another.

"Don't talk like that. He's Sammy's boyfriend. Well, at least he will be in a minute now that she's been properly prepped." Sammy took this opportunity to expel gas from a second orifice.

Maryanne returned with my drink. “You’re getting your dog drunk so another dog can have sex with her? That’s disgusting.”

“It’s how I got you.”

“It is ...” she halted her denial mid sentence. “Well that was different though.”

I just waved my hand at her. Clearly dismissive. I very much like being dismissive and through the years I have developed quite a talent for it. As well I can show disdain but this seems less effective. I led a wobbly Sammy to the door and sent her out to join her companion, refilled my drink, and plopped down on my recliner to watch some television.

"Underneath this flabby exterior is an enormous lack of character."

Oscar Levant

I changed into my favorite pair of baggy bermudas and a flannel shirt, unbuttoned for maximum comfort of course, and slid on some long, white tube socks to keep my gnarled toes warm. I referred to it as my 'grandpa mowing the lawn look'. Maryanne preferred to call it my 'aging fat and lazy fuck attire'. Regardless of its name I was quite comfortable, leaning back on my couch, sipping my bourbon.

Maryanne looked less comfortable. She was in the recliner, by now very gimpy eyed and drunk. She would appear to pass out then pop awake and hurl profanities and crudities at Rush Limbaugh, who's porcine countenance graced my Sony. Exhausting herself after a few sentences she would slump back in the chair, as if someone had pulled her power supply out of the wall socket. Occasional howls and squeals from the backyard interrupted our domestic bliss. Then she was awake again, looking as if she might puke but having no intention of running to the toilet.

"Your dog is being raped." She offered with a sibilant sound created by excess saliva.

"She's not being raped."

"Then what would you call it?"

"Sexual assault, reckless endangerment maybe. Certainly not rape. OR MAYBE ITS JUST CALLED BREEDING MY FUCKING DOG." Maryanne was serving nicely as a substitute for a pet at which to scream.

The problem with people, however, is that they talk back. Maryanne threw her half - filled glass at the wall and shattered it. There was by now quite a decent pile of broken shards of glass littering my floor.

"What did you do that for? We only throw kitchenware at pets in this house."

The toss had sapped her energy and her strength. "You have spots on your wall."

"I know. Because people keep throwing full drinks at it."

"Not those kind of spots. Black spots, and they move around."

"I think those spots are in your head."

"No Jay, I'm serious. Not spots really. More like dark blobs of nothingness. A wet void seeping out of the frame of the house. They darken then disappear, then come back somewhere else. Only they come back larger and darker, like this house is slowly being pulled into some endless abyss."

I squinted and peered at my white walls. If I looked hard enough I could begin to see the blobs. Ebbing and flowing like a lava lamp. My entire house slowly being swept up in a growing, wet blackness. Then I opened my eyes and the house appeared normal again. Maryanne snored rather unappealingly in my recliner, a small mucous bubble forming in her left nostril. The doorbell rang.

I staggered to the door and answered it. Mandy Davis, my next door neighbor, was staring at my exposed belly, which I was scratching casually with my right hand, the index finger of which absently explored my bellybutton.

Mandy is small and young and cute. At least she would be cute if her face wasn't constantly scrunched up in an expression that gave me the impression she was always trying to pinch the head off a canary with her anal sphincter. I'm guessing this woman takes no more than a single bowel movement per month and even that often is distasteful to her. She was wearing a warm - up suit, her frosted hair pulled back in a tourniquet tight pony - tail, bangs hanging free, her face heavily made up even at this late hour.

"Dr. Day, you know I'm not a busybody or anything like that . . .".

I cut her off. "Call me Jordan." I dug some lint from my bellybutton and eyed it warily, speculating as to its source.

"Jordan, its just that my little Cody can't get any sleep. We hear screams and glass breaking and those dogs howling. You have to show some consideration." Cody is a vicious and hideous infant, always nattily dressed in Baby Gap togs. He has spit on me once and peed on me three times. I think under orders from his parents.

I should have been polite and apologetic at this point, and I did try. I'm just not very good at those particular things. "I'm really sorry Mandy. It has just been a crazy day. Would you like to come in for a quick drink?" I motioned her inside while wiping my lint covered index finger on the door frame.

Mandy looked inside uncomfortably, searching for my Really Big Dog, and appeared as if she might accept. At that moment Maryanne rolled rightward in the recliner, reached for the potted plant on the floor next to her, and vomited violently.

Mandy backed slowly away from the door. Dainty hands with painted fingernails covered her mouth and her button nose. She was entirely speechless so I decided to speak. "Maybe now isn't the best time. I'll try to keep it down though." I shut the door as Mandy continued her slow retreat.

I took the besoiled plant and placed it outside in the backyard. I noticed that Sammy was darting around and yelping, looking very much like a drunken and caged psychotic. Shakespeare just gave me an exasperated look. I shrugged my shoulders to let him know I understood, then returned to the safety of my home.

I had been seated comfortably for all of two minutes, checking to make sure that Maryanne wasn't aspirating, when an earth moving thud resounded throughout the house. I pulled back the curtain and saw my Really Big Dog charging head first for another shot at the glass door. She struck it with such force that cracks spiderwebbed their way from the center of impact. The noise startled Maryanne, who rolled out of the recliner and struck her left eye rather convincingly against the end table.

Maryanne began screaming and sobbing, a trickle of blood coming down her face, the swelling already beginning. I struggled to help her to a seated position. As I did this Sammy rammed the window again and began to howl. Maryanne screamed as well.

"RAPE. That beast is trying to rape your dog. STOP IT NOW."

I went to my medical bag and grabbed a little Ativan to sedate the dog. I managed to corral her and gave her a quick shot in the butt. I held her big head in my arms and checked for damage. The sedative had its effect and My Really Big Dog calmed and then slept, her skull apparently intact.

I went back inside to attend to Maryanne who had taken to vomiting again. She recovered and even laughed a little. Then another knock on the door. I started to move to answer it when Maryanne started screaming again. "RAPE, RAPE. STOP IT JAY, YOU GOTTA STOP IT. ITS RAPE."

I looked outside the window and saw that Shakespeare had sensed an opportunity with the comatose Sammy. He was mounted and doing his business. I tried to break them up but a peculiarity of canine anatomy makes them extremely difficult to separate while involved in the act. Shakespeare howled in pain. Maryanne howled in horror, I just howled, and the police burst through my front door, splintering the frame where my stomach lint had recently found a home.

The Wal-Mart Chronicles . . .

"Don't let it end like this, tell them I said something."

Last words of Pancho Villa

"I don't feel good."

Last words of Luther Burbank

The home into which the police burst stunk of alcohol and vomit. A used syringe was sitting in open sight on the kitchen counter. My girlfriend was bleeding and developing a shiner. She was incoherent and mumbling things about rape and wet black spots, clearly traumatized. I was witnessed in an unnatural position with a large dog and Maryanne mentioned early on that I'd gotten said dog drunk. Seemingly hundreds of neighbors were outside, bathed in swirling lights, relating strange comings and goings at my house, the frequent yelling and sounds of violence that came from my walls. The shattering glass and odd howls that had been going on all evening. A shifty character that had appeared in a pick - up then sped off into the night, probably after having purchased narcotics from the slovenly doctor . The doctor's obvious disregard for proper yard care.

I tried several times to relate my side of the story but could never get past the gin in the dog bowl or the broken glasses on the floor or the used syringe. I finally quit and accepted handcuffs quietly. Maryanne was hustled off to a hospital that had a rape crisis unit. I was led through my throng of neighbors who alternately cheered and yelled obscenities. I snarled back for a while then tired and quit, beaten. My Really Big Dog slept peacefully in the back yard.

Candy was just looking at me as I finished my story, not questioning a word of it. She patted me on my bald head. "So I guess you're really just some kind of moron, that's all." I nodded my head. I knew she'd understand. Candy went on, "Lucky for you that's not against the law."

"They put me in prison for it."

"Not prison Sammy, jail." We sat silently for a few moments.

"You never told me what happened to Shakespeare."

I smiled. I smiled because I didn't really know. I knew he got out of my yard and had run off. I laughed because I imagined that he'd snatched up little Cody in his huge jaws and taken him off to the wilds.

Candy grinned at me and put my bald head back on her shoulder.

Hypothermia

Chapter 1: Hi There

I am standing in her house now. The floor is aged hardwood and there are loose boards that creak as I shift my weight uncomfortably, something I seem to be doing quite a bit. She seems very small as she stands in front of me, holding a HUGE glass of wine in both hands, the burgundy liquid sloshing dangerously as she talks.

Her boney shoulders are hunched forward as she looks up at me, like she is trying to hide the fact that she has breasts, hide that she is, in fact, a woman. A white short sleeve sweater hangs loosely on her frame, barely reaching her waist, it's threads rough and unraveling slightly.

"This is it" she says. "My home. You like?" She is waving her arm around the house, gesturing grandly, showing it off, not quite proud.

I don't know her at all, not really, and I have no idea what to think of her house. It seems nice but cluttered and old with low ceilings and narrow hallways, built in a different time for a different sized people. The curtains are whitish and they diffuse all the light in the room. Everything seems hazy and indistinct, objects lack edges. Beginnings and endings aren't clear. It looks like it is being shot with a hand held camera through a gauzy filter - an afternoon movie on the Lifetime Network.

I said I don't know her at all and that is true - except it isn't. I know her in pieces. I have encountered fragments of her but never experienced the whole. I tended not to think of her as a physical entity. In my mind she was simply assigned a screen name and a random icon.

She found me in cyberspace somehow - started sending me IMs and emails, never telling me that she saw me most days at the hospital, at least in passing. Never telling me that we had even exchanged nods and perhaps a "hello". I figured it out slowly.

There was a "realness" to her online persona - a depth and texture that people in the actual world so often lack. She had a presence and a sense of humor. She was large and forceful and impossible to ignore.

I'm sure she thought I was all those things too - large and forceful and deep - but I am not. She first saw me at work, in the ER, and thought THAT was really me, that I was commanding and sure of myself, that I told other people what to do and they did it, that I had some meager insight into the human condition, that I wore starched white coats and squeaky bright orange clogs, that

I smelled of digested blood and alcohol based hand cleanser, that I had access to prescription narcotics and was privy to some sort of secret knowledge about the vagina, that I could somehow fix what was wrong with people. She definitely got the wrong impression.

I asked her to dinner one night while we were playing cribbage online. She asked if we could just "skip the dinner part".

So now I am here, having stepped through the computer monitor only to find a world just like my own, populated by the same sad characters. Her name is Laura and she is a receptionist (admissions specialist actually) at the hospital where I work. She is age-appropriate as my niece would say, somewhere in her early 30's. She supposedly has a 3 year old boy roaming around here. He is probably skullking behind a chair waiting to attack me with dirty diapers and a bad attitude.

She is almost very pretty but her head is enormous and her shoulders and arms thin and frail. She looks as if she might topple over from the sheer weight of her bulbous noggin. She looks the way many actresses do in real life - distorted and cartoonish and lacking proportion, a beauty built only to live inside a camera.

Faded jeans are slung low on her hips and a pierced navel is visible when her gestures cause her sweater to rise up. Peeking up from behind her belt, paws extended as if escaping from her nether regions, is a tattoo of a gray mouse, running from the kitty I suppose. Such things can be omens but I am apt to miss them.

She is seeing me in a new light as well, no longer a doctor or a boss but an overweight middle-aged guy that is slowly losing his hair and who keeps his shirts untucked because he thinks that this hides his waistline. Huge in some ways, 6'6" and 260 pounds, I move with a cowardice and fear. I seem strangely small and unintimidating, as if my reluctant persona somehow actually causes this giant body to take up less space in the physical world.

Laura takes a deep breath and gulps more wine. Her tongue darts out like an amphibious predator to catch a stray drop caught in the downy hair above her lip.

Chapter 2: The Meal

Laura is cooking now, her promise to "skip dinner" apparently forgotten. Her 3 year old son, Hunter, is stomping on my left foot and letting out lispy yelps, marking his territory like a deranged midget.

There are other children, or there should be. Laura has an older son and daughter but they don't live with her and haven't for a long time. She has said little about it, only that her second husband, Hunter's father, is to blame. He seems to be to blame for quite a bit.

I rise to try and help her carry plates, and to remove myself from the grips of her elfin devil. As I approach her she starts just a little, like a flinch, as if half expecting some kind of blow. She smiles up at me meekly, embarrassed.

The food is chicken enchiladas. I am starting to believe there is some kind of culinary school for single women who can't cook and the instructors chant at these ladies to "Melt some cheese - just smother it in CHEESE!" It is a not bad strategy.

I am uncomfortable eating at other people's houses. Uncomfortable, in fact, eating food prepared by other people - unless the food arrives via a drive-thru window. I'm not sure why this is. I am not fastidious or even picky. Maybe I am somehow convinced folks want to poison me.

I am picking at my food, making swirls in the pools of oil that are congealing around the beans and cheese. Thinking that perhaps this woman is fattening me for slaughter. Laura is noticing this. She is scarfing down large mouthfuls that I can only assume she will barf up later in the accepted fashion of modern women. I make a note to offer her gum if I decide to kiss her.

"You don't like it?" she asks, her voice muffled a bit because her mouth is full.

"No, it's good" I lie unconvincingly. "I just have a sort of thing with food, an uncomfortable relationship with it I guess."

She rolls her eyes. "Don't we all".

"I mean that I think about the food too much. Where it comes from. What it looks like." I say "A meal prepared by someone else comes with baggage. It contains thoughts and expectations from the preparer."

"This meal contains chicken and cheese" she says. "And hopefully no pieces of plastic from when I took off the microwave safe cover."

I am soothed by this, happy that my food was probably prepared by underpaid and illegal day laborers hundreds of miles away and then flash frozen for transport in big trucks that have mud flaps with pictures of naked girls. I like that my food is part of an industry, mass produced and chemically treated. All food should be this impersonal.

"You have good nuking skills" I say.

"I try" she answers. "I learned from my mom. I come from a family of microwavers. For a while we experimented with convection ovens and George Foreman grills but the results didn't satisfy. The food lacked the essential rubbery-ness of properly irradiated cuisine."

I am oddly aroused by this confession. I want to know more about her upbringing surrounded by Chef Boyardee and hot dogs with frayed and crispy ends.

Laura finishes her food and excuses herself to the bathroom. I cover my ears to hide the sounds of her retching or tinkling or whatever she is doing. I prefer to imagine that my women don't produce waste products.

"My mom is coming over" she says when she returns. "Did I mention that? She is going to pick up Hunter. Babysit."

No, she hadn't mentioned that.

Chapter 3: The Boy

The boy, Hunter, is the center of everything. Even when he is asleep or absent he is at the forefront - of thought and conversation and concern. He is an odd looking child, too much forehead and too little fat. He isn't appropriately chubby for a 3 year old - no subcutaneous adipose. His face and body have shapes and angles that seem more appropriate for an adult. His skin sags in places, lacking the rubbery vigor of the very young. Plus he curses a lot.

He seems precocious in some ways and retarded in others, a result of spending huge chunks of his short life in the hospital. Sick kids develop language and adult personas very early. Emotionally they aren't stunted, but they accept a depth of sadness that is out of proportion. They are comfortable with the pain and disappointment life dishes out. Little soldiers.

Hunter had a rare congenital anomaly. I like that term "congenital anomaly". It takes the sting out of what it really is - a devastating birth defect. I enjoy language like this - language that comforts and soothes while obscuring meaning. It is language as a weapon, coaxing the enemy into a psychic space that we can absorb, deal with, tolerate.

He had a large abdominal aortic aneurysm. A weakening and ballooning of the largest artery in his body. This is a fairly common, if at times devastating, condition in the elderly. In adults an aneurysm is followed by ultrasound until it reaches a certain size, 5 cm usually. At this size it is believed that the risk of rupture is greater than the risk of surgery or stenting to repair it. Rupture is often fatal, even if it occurs IN the hospital the mortality is 50% or so. It seems to hurt quite a bit, rupture that is. Abdominal aneurysms are almost unheard of in children. I didn't believe Laura when she told me. I thought she misunderstood or something.

They found it almost by accident when he was 8 months old. He was a smallish and sickly neonate. Crying all the time and not feeding well. "Failure to thrive" they call it, another beautiful use of language. They looked for the cause but found nothing, until someone checked his blood pressure and noticed it was 200/110, wildly high.

The search for the cause of the blood pressure led to imaging - CTs and arteriography. Snapshots of his entire body, procured by radiation and magnetism and dye. Modern witchcraft. They saw it then, impossible to miss.

He was started on medicine to keep his blood pressure low, meds to protect his kidneys, flown to Cleveland for a second opinion. He had a major surgery, his abdomen opened from diaphragm to pubis, intestines pushed out of the way with retractors, the aneurysm resected and patched with space age materials. Good as new.

Except for the issue of WHY. Why did a baby have an aneurysm? Opinions differed. Maybe it was an isolated problem. Perhaps he had a genetic error in which his body didn't make connective tissue properly, produced defective collagen. Nobody knew - or knows.

They think he is okay for now - except as he grows the patch will become inadequate and will need to be replaced, probably several times before he is an adult, each surgery with a small but very real risk of death. And then there is the worry of other aneurysms, in other vessels, developing. Every pain or illness a possible warning sign. His mother obsessively checking his blood pressure, tracking it in a notebook 4 times a day.

Waiting for the other shoe to drop.

Chapter 4: The Pills

Laura's mother stumbles into the house like someone trying to escape the rain. She is wearing tennis shoes and jean shorts and an enormous varicose vein bulges behind her right knee. I can't take my eyes off its snakey edges. It throbs and bends and surely must explode but never does.

She oozes busy-ness, this woman does. She is kinetic, hyperactive, vibrating at an almost molecular level. Her left shoe is untied and she stumbles and rams her petrified hair extensions into a paper thin wall that almost gives way.

"Greetings" she says to me. "Are you the rented penis?"

"I'm not sure" I stammer. "Nobody has paid me yet." I am pleased with my response. I feel witty and urbane.

"You should speak less, Mr. Penis" her mother goes on. "You're kinda cute until you speak. Light my cigarette?"

She leans towards me with a thin foreign smoke between painted lips, strands of the thick lipstick cling to the end of the cigarette as it dangles slightly. She smells strongly of rum and hair gel.

I look at the boy, Hunter, standing by the wall, trying to wedge his tongue into an electrical outlet. I'm wondering if smoking around this kid is wise. I decide it doesn't matter, he went past three strikes a while ago. He may as well get to enjoy the pleasures of second hand smoking.

I nearly set her hair on fire when I ignite my Zippo. She is teetering forward, unsteady and unable to center her cigarette in the flame. She grabs my wrist and holds it, as if it is ME that is swaying in and out of range. A smudge of black ash becomes visible on her cheek. She looks like a person that has just escaped a house fire.

I stand to introduce myself formally but she waves me back down to my seat, through with me for now. Laura is just standing in the shadows, blushing. The pair of them excuse themselves to the kitchen, mumbling in witless conspiracy.

I have recently quit smoking but have been looking for a reason to start again. I carry a pack and my lighter everywhere, enjoying the temptation and the small victory of deprivation. I determine that this is as good a time as any to resume my slow suicide.

My cigarette smells heavenly and I offer one to 3 year old Hunter but he is busy pulling his shorts down and peeing in the corner. I voice my encouragement, unconditional positive regard being a centerpiece to my child rearing theories.

"Having a 3 year old in the house is EXACTLY like having a very short drunk hanging around" I say to noone in particular. The women look up for a moment but then return to rummaging in each other's purses. Hunter turns from the wall, looks at me, then pukes. I throw a piece of newspaper over his mess like I used to do with my cats. Hunter neglects to thank me.

I am sitting at the kitchen bar now, wanting to join the other grown ups in conversation but it seems they think I have little to offer. Prescription bottles litter the counter and mother and daughter are examining the labels, comparing milligrams and dosing intervals.

There are antidepressants of numerous types. Pain meds, sedatives, and anxiolytics. "Fibromyalgia" they both say at once. I just nod. There are meds for ulcers and meds to speed digestion as well as something for cramping and something for nausea. "Irritable Bowel Syndrome" says her mother and pats her slight pooch.

I nod again "All the cheese probably" I say.

They both just look at me as you would a dirty panhandler.

They are sampling pills like they are at a tasting of fine cheeses. They take a nibble of a Vicodin and a "chip" off a Xanax bar. They sniff a Phenergan then wash it down with a gulp of wine to cleanse the pallet. Laura digs through her purse for some "diet" pills and what looks like Ritalin. They whisper something to each other and decide to take one of each to combat the sedation.

"We're being rude" Laura says to her mother and they both turn to me. "Did you want some?"

"I'm alright" I say. "My fibromyalgia is currently in remission. Do you have any REAL drugs? Illegal stuff. Coke, pot, heroin, X. I'm kind of a traditionalist."

"Viagra is what you need Mr. Penis" says my date's mother. "I advise taking two."

Chapter 5: Scale

I'm sitting with the boy, Hunter, now - or trying to. Laura's mother has come by to pick him up, babysit for the evening. Laura and her mother have disappeared, giggling and drinking wine and discussing bizarre and inappropriate things like panties and birth control and scented soaps. So here I sit with the boy.

He has a plastic bat and he is swatting things. He is small but doesn't seem fragile. He knocks a book off a table and says "shit!" quite clearly as it hits the ground. He says "dammit!" when he trips and falls. Otherwise his speech is tough to decipher. If he wants something he points and grunts or maybe whines. He can say "hungry" and "eat" and "wet" but is strangely silent when it comes to naming THINGS, like the part of his brain that processes nouns is somehow damaged or malfunctioning. He is mostly a descriptive lad.

I want to tell him things. Explain to him about certain hard and fast facts in this world, information he wouldn't get from his mom or grandmother. Tell him manly stuff. Fill his small brain with data and detail to counter the effeminate world he knows. I want him to know things are CONNECTED to one another.

Except I don't really know how to talk to kids. I find them to be poor listeners. Self involved. Moody. Obsessively literal. Adding very little of true substance. Also they are often covered in snot and drool.

So I just start talking. I talk about the bat he is holding and move on to bats in general. I tell him about the different woods and weights - the hardiness of ash versus the power and fragility of maple, the controversy of metal. I talk about the physics of corking, the importance of bat speed and the hitting zone. I ramble about the rituals of hitting, Willie Stargell's bat twirl, Joe Morgan's elbow flap, Pete Rose's crouch, the importance of sameness in the swing, little affectations that batters develop for timing.

I talk about distances, about how baseball measures things in feet. The bases are 90 feet apart - always. I tell him that you can figure out the distance from home plate to 2nd base because we know the length of 2 sides of the triangle. I tell him that there is a formula for this, that smart dudes figured out the formula long ago, realized that the world was full of fixed ratios and that through careful logic we could deduce facts from observations with absolute accuracy. I told him the distance from Home to 2nd was about 127.28 feet. Distance to the fences varies, short down the line - deep in center.

"Shit" says Hunter and throws a Frito to the ground and stomps on it.

"Well said Hunter" I say, "It IS bothersome that all outfields are different. But it's part of the "character" of the game. During the '70s some people experimented with fairly uniform ballparks. Busch Stadium, Three Rivers in Pittsburgh, Riverfront in Cincinnatti - these stadiums were almost indistinguishable once you went inside. They had astroturf and it was like watching guys play on green concrete. That didn't work out so well. Sometimes you could see ripples and worn places in the carpet. The world turned on astroturf pretty quickly. One year it was the BIG new thing, the next it was the Devil's own surface. The world is that way - moody."

Hunter vomits up some coagulated cheese, smacking his lips as if savoring the aftertaste. I ignore this.

"You need to pay attention to numbers" I say. "Numbers are beautifully descriptive. They are exact and reproducible. They translate well. They can be adjusted and manipulated to find other numbers. For instance a kilogram is equal to the mass of one liter of water. This is 2.2 pounds by the way but the pound isn't equal to the weight of anything. It is just a pound. I find that disappointing. The metric system is beautiful that way - beautiful in it's logic, it's symmetry."

"Pay attention to units" I say. "Numbers mean little without units. Inches or centimeters or yards or gallons. Numbers become relative without units and lose their power, the power of exactness, of indisputability."

"Be accurate in your measurements" I say as he picks up the vomited cheese and stares at it. "Numbers are only worthwhile if they are accurate and reproducible. Take PRIDE in your ability to measure and record, it separates us from other species."

Hunter nods at this and makes monkey sounds, hopping around on one foot and scratching his privates. His understanding obvious.

"Numbers ARE reality" I say. "If you understand numbers and ratios and scale then the universe becomes knowable and finite. The free throw line is 15 feet on a basketball court, on ALL basket ball courts. If you need to estimate a distance just picture in your mind a known quantity like the free throw line or a football field. This offers perspective. The top of the key is 20 ft. Halfcourt is 47 feet. Baseline to baseline 94 feet. Football fields are 100 yards (note the unit change) except in Canada and that isn't worth discussing. Or maybe it is worth discussing because Canadian football lacks credibility BECAUSE their field is non-standard, BECAUSE the numbers don't translate."

Hunter runs full speed and lowers his head, ramming me like a very weak missile. There is a gentle “thwack” and he backs up, teetering a little and giggling. “Shit” he says. Then adds “I’m thwee”.

“Yes you are” I say. “Three years. That’s a unit of time. Our units of time are a little screwy. 60 minutes in an hour, 24 hours in a day, 7 days in a week, 365+ days in a year, 60 seconds in a minute. This is a bad system. When we move under one second we get better, move to a base 10 system, break the time down into tenths and hundredths and thousands and on and on. This makes sense. The prefixes become familiar and easy to manage, MILLIsecond, NANOsecond. That is language as description. Language as it was meant to be. Language that illuminates.”

Hunter is spinning around in circles now. He spins until he gets dizzy and then he wobbles and falls. He gets up and spins again. He falls and he cries.

I say, “I know what you mean, man. I know what you mean.”

Chapter 6: Memory of Magic

My evening is morphing into something strange and unplanned. Laura's mother, who I have taken to referring to as "Broomhilda" in my head, has plopped into the recliner and removed her tennis shoes, wiggling her toes in grimey white ankle socks. It appears she may not be going anywhere for awhile.

The boy has gone to bed, dreaming of furry things and anesthetics and the freedom to put his tongue on random objects. He has his own iPod and it is playing some kind of "white noise" that is supposed to be soothing but strikes me more as the soundtrack of the decline of civilization. The buzzing of the end of thought.

Broomhilda took another "chip" of xanax and has started snoring in her chair, her half full glass of wine balanced precariously on her leg. She has just finished regaling us with stories about her 25 year-old "lover" and what seems like an extensive, fairly tiring and frankly kinda gross sex life.

Laura has become liquid. Not quite drunk, not quite stoned she is graceful now, living in the split second, her ability to think deeply and form memories displaced by pharmacological genius. She is scratching my scalp and picking at my hair, like a chimp grooming it's mate.

She is whispering in my ear. Whispering about food and wine and how "smooth" she feels. She whispers about her grief.

There is something appealing in her sadness, something life affirming about her fear of the next day. Her grief has come alive. She embodies it to such an extent that she is inseparable from it. It exists in her movement and her gestures. Even her laughter is sad.

"Benzodiazepines" she says. "That's what Xanax is. It's drug class. It's chemical essence. Valium, Versed, Ativan, Klonopin. These are all benzodiazepines. Given for anxiety and seizures and alcohol withdrawal. Used for conscious sedation during painful procedures. They are like magic."

I want to tell her that I know all of this. That this is my business. But I like hearing her talk about it. Her voice has the poetry of hard won knowledge.

"GABA receptors, that's where they work. In the brain. I like that name GABA. GABA is a neurotransmitter - a chemical signal between neurons. We think it inhibits or maybe slows things down. Benzos somehow make GABA more effective - potentiate it is what they say. That's another good word - potentiate.

"Benzos stabilize cell membranes - like that means anything. Somehow they keep electrical charge from spreading neuron to neuron. That is how they stop seizures. By stabilizing the membranes - by stopping the propagation of waves of electricity in the brain, spreading from a focus like wildfire from a cigarette.

"They cause memory problems the same way. This isn't well understood but memories reside briefly in the "short-term" area. Like a holding cell while the brain prepares it's permanent home, develops associations and fellow travelers, files it correctly or incorrectly. How this filing occurs isn't clear. Perhaps a group of cells are slightly modified by transmitters binding to them. This isn't known. What is known is that neurotransmitters are involved, that GABA receptors are involved.

"The benzos seem to make it so the memories won't stick. They inhibit the firing of the neurons that etch things in permanence, so that things park in short-term memory but never get moved to long-term, or it is possible that they DO get moved but they get misplaced or misfiled - associated with the wrong smells and sounds. Again - this isn't clear. It seems more likely though that the memory never gets formed at all. Reality just bounces off a teflon brain, unable to make a stable connection."

She has her head in my lap now and I am petting her hair. She smells of wine and Velveeta with a hint of dirty socks wafting through the air. I picture reality bouncing off the smooth shell of her brain like a Nerf missile striking a football helmet. I imagine the bliss of her amnesia.

"There is a theory", I say, "that before Shakespeare, English speaking peoples were not capable of romantic love."

"That's silly" she answers. "Physiologically there is no difference between people then and people now. Except maybe we are taller and fatter. And they probably smelled really bad, what with the lack of toilet paper and all."

"The difference wouldn't be physiologic" I say. "At least not primarily. The difference is language and the extent to which language controls thought. Abstract ideas are difficult to impossible without language. Words give us concrete ways to think about things - and to pass those ideas on from generation to generation. Language allows us to transmit the INFORMATION of ideas and knowledge from person to person, much like DNA allows us to transfer the information of our biology. They even have a name for the ideas that get transferred. They call them "Memes". Kind of like "genes" but not so much."

Laura belches gently into her palm and I offer her a stick of gum. She declines but I insist. Her belch smells like decomposing enchiladas. "What do memes have to do with romantic love?"

"Romance is an idea. It isn't biological. Biology insists on sex and reproduction. Romance is a story, a fiction our big brains build around this biologic imperative. A story that makes it all more palatable and possibly more efficient - improving offspring by giving them happy parents or maybe parents that stick around to raise them longer. I'm not really sure. I am only sure that it is a useful fiction that likely has value to our species.

"The idea of romance is a meme. Given to us by Shakespeare in large part. Can you guess the origin of the word "meme"."

Laura is smoking now, the cigarettes stolen from her passed out mother. "I'll assume it has the same origin as "memory"."

She hands me the cigarette and I take a drag from it, as if we are sharing a joint. The filter is moist with her saliva and I imagine how she might taste. "Basically yeah. Memes are group memories or group thoughts."

She starts talking again but I'm not sure she understands she is speaking out loud. "Without memories there is no fear - no anxiety. I think this is one of the ways benzos work. It becomes impossible to chew on information, on fears because I can't hold thoughts in my head long enough."

"Fear and anxiety are side effects of memory" I say. "Maladaptive off-shoots. Unintended consequences. Language and memory make us stronger as a people, as a species. But they plague and hinder some individuals."

"What was the point of this again? The point about romantic love? I can't remember." She is mumbling now, barely intelligible.

"Wiping out memories can be a cure for fear and anxiety" I say, whispering it lightly in her ear. "But without memory there is no love. We become 2 dimensional, flat like notebook paper or bad photographs. We lose the depth that is the only thing that makes us interesting."

I wait for a response but realize one is not coming. She is sleeping now. It wouldn't matter anyway. She won't remember.

Chapter 7: Monkeys

Laura is sleeping now, or maybe just resting. She seems to rouse every ten or fifteen minutes to spit and grumble unintelligibly. I was going to carry her to bed but in the end this struck me far to chivalrous so I just shook her and threw a night shirt her way.

Tucked under the covers she seems younger but at the same time far more broken. She is small and weak and her hair is a mess and her breath is bad and her lipstick is smeared. She is 34 years old and faces 15 years of caring for a perennially sick child. She makes somewhere around 8 bucks an hour.

Outside her bedroom window the summer night is building to a storm. Wind lashes her screen doors and debris brushes the glass. Hunks of hail or heavy raindrops THUD on the roof like we are under attack. I adore weather like this. I crawl under the covers and lay my head on her shoulder, listening to her breathe. Tornado sirens keen in the distance.

The boy is awake now, frightened by the thunder. He is standing up in his crib, shaking the bars like an inmate demanding release. His cries are steady, measured, insistent.

Mom and Grandma are too drunk and medicated to respond so I leave the bed and walk to his room. There are murals of bears and baseball players painted in pastels on the walls and in the dark and the flashes of lightning they seem to startle and move and freak me out more than a little.

Hunter waves to me, unperturbed by his walls coming to life.

I lift him from the crib and he smells of urine and wet dog. His belly hangs over his diaper and he has folds in his arms and a scar on his chest. I tell him that he looks out of shape, that he needs to work out more, change his diet. He seems to understand but maybe not completely.

I sit on the floor and lean back against the wall, unsure of what one does with a frightened child in the middle of the night. It occurs to me that I should simply put him back to bed but this seems silly.

He is a whirling dervish. Zipped from sleep to full speed in under 5 minutes. He is throwing stuff around the room as if on a treasure hunt. He looks to be like a monkey marking his territory. His gait has that slight side to side sway and each movement is deliberate and exaggerated, a tumbling momentum gained after a few steps.

"I think we should have baby exhibits in zoos" I tell him. "Put you guys in your natural habitat of flannel and gruel and car seats but keep us adults at a safe distance, behind a fence and maybe a moat. These are the sorts of things I think about."

Hunter is sidling up to me. Touching my big nose with his little fingers, his sharp thumbnail possibly drawing blood from my nostril. He smiles and plops down.

"Childless adults could go observe you guys behave in the wild" I say. "Learn and be entertained at the same time. ' LOOK' we'll say, 'they touch themselves just like monkeys.' Keepers will hose out your pen twice a day to keep it fresh and neat. You will be fed through gigantic straws and rewarded with Pez."

The boy is rapidly losing interest and looks like he might cry. I find the changing table and flop him up there like a rag doll. He giggles like a villain. I tell him a story while I lift him by the legs and wipe his bottom with a damp cloth.

"I've always wanted to build a giant house" I say to him. "No, not a really big house, I mean like a house where a GIANT would live. The doors would all be 12 feet and the ceilings 20. I would need a step ladder to get into the recliner or crawl on the couch. Everything will be huge, it will swallow me.

"The kitchen table will be chest high and the bar eye level. My feet will dangle from the chairs and the plates will be the size of serving platters. Even the silverware will be huge and clumsy.

"This house will shrink me. It will make me small and insignificant, forever a child in a world of grown ups."

Hunter is just staring at me now. Happy and clean in his new diaper.

"You can come hang out at my Giant House" I say. "It'll have a giant tv. We can disappear together."

Chapter 8: Fear

Hunter is back in his crib now. He snores like an old man when he sleeps, half bubbles of snot forming at his nostril. I try to wipe his face but this makes him start to cry so I let it go and listen to him snuffle and sputter. It is rhythmic and exaggerated and calming.

When I am sure he is down I walk out into the dark house. Moonlight half brightens the front two rooms. Broomhilda is blanketed in stark shadows - the left half of her sleeping face darkened. It seems lifeless, like she has stroked out there on the couch. I see a stray Frito sitting on the table and I pick it up and lob it at her. She doesn't stir.

I move to the front window and watch the neighborhood move through its middle of the night rituals. This street is suburban in the extreme - starter houses on small lots with curvy, cul-de-sacked streets. For Sale signs dot the yards like lawn ornaments. Scattered lots are under construction and mid-sod. One house has a big wheeled truck at the curb and an old Camaro in the driveway. The car is decorated with about 15 floppy antennas. The residents are sitting in the open garage with lawn chairs and a cooler, unidentifiable music thumping faintly through the still damp air.

The occasional pair of headlights weaves drunkenly homeward, the splash of its tires making an audible Doppler effect as they whoosh slowly by. A hunched, furtive man wheels garbage can after garbage can to his curb then staggers out under the weight of a large rolled up carpet. I wonder if he is disposing of the wife piece by piece. I glance over at Broomhilda and think to myself it is best not to be TOO judgmental in cases of domestic homicide.

I move back into the house, into the darkness and start down the long hallway. It is "L" shaped and goes past the two bedrooms I have seen as well as a second bathroom that reeks of incense and guest soap. I feel like a burglar or a peeping Tom or maybe even a very shy and ineffectual rapist. At the end of the short arm of the "L" is another large room - perhaps supposed to be a guest room or an office or a library. It is none of these things though I am not sure WHAT to call it.

I flick the light switch and flourescents flicker alive. A SHITHOLE, I decide. This room is intended to be some sort of DUNG HEAP that collects the waste products of the rest of the house – sort of its Large Intestine where the feces wait while they are partially dehydrated and packaged together as managable chunks.

There are piles of paper everywhere. The biggest piles cover nearby and seemingly weaker piles adjacent to them. Sheets of looseleaf infiltrate neighboring notebooks willy-nilly.

Folders of various types lie scattered about, defeated and broken by their overwhelming content they look old and sad and weathered.

I notice that some of the folders contain x-rays, the plastic corners crinkled and stained with drips of coffee. This shithole, this office, begins to look more like a hideously disorganized medical records filing room.

There are innumerable doctor's dictations scattered about. There are reports of x-rays and CT scans and MRIs and Ultrasounds. There are Histories and Physicals and there are Discharge Summaries and Progress Notes. There are physical copies of the scans themselves, a couple have been framed though not hung. There are only two patients represented here – Hunter and Laura herself. The records for the boy showing disease of some kind from the day he was born. Those of Laura are almost as abundant but they show nothing but the glory of good protoplasm, perfect health and exquisite numbers. She seems almost like a control group that is being compared to the experiment in modern health and materials that is Hunter.

This is a room that is filled with a modern interpretation of human kind. People are digitized and flattened and made anonymous. We become our ailments. The print outs of the MRIs are a series of 2 dimensional "slices" that our minds reconstruct as 3 dimensional. The images themselves are also indirect, the computer is sensing the density of hydrogen atoms, tempoarily polarized by a giant magnet. The algorithim then infers the water content and density of each layer of tissue based on the amount of hydrogen in each spot. These densities are represented by lighter and darker colors, denser being lighter by convention and could just as easily be reversed by the flick of a switch. We are about 4 layers removed from direct observation here yet it seems as if we can see ourselves EXACTLY as we are.

Many of the papers contain lab values and these have a pleasant and comforting association for me. Labs and numbers remind of work and school and things finite and measurable. Thyroid levels, potassium, sodium, calcium, BUN, creatinine, B-12, Folate, hemoglobin, hematocrit, amylase, lipase, lipid levels, oxygen saturations, C-reactive protein, ANA, RF, tick panels, hepatitis screens from A to E. Some of these values are calculated by combining several of the others. Abnormal values are marked with yellow highliter.

I walk slowly around the room and look at this medical abstraction, a depiction of human life as numbers or computer extrapolations. There is a scan of Hunter's aneurysm - before and after. There is an MRI of his brain with bright colors showing normal function but perhaps some frontal lobe atrophy. Laura's spine is vivid in sharply contrasted shades of gray. Her uterus and ovaries, with fibroids and cysts, almost pulsate from a Cat Scan and Ultrasound. Her skull comes across as a spooky halloween mask in a series of coronal sections.

"It keeps me warm" Laura's voice comes from behind me. "Sometimes I feel like I'm freezing to death – but from the inside out. Like I have somehow become hypothermic at my core." She is standing in the doorway watching me look at this version of her family. "My fears seem to warm me. It helps to keep your fears close to your heart."

I don't say anything. It is almost spectacular as well as blindingly sad, allaying anxieties about death and pain through pointless obsession.

"It gives it a face" she goes on, her voice hoarse and phlegmy from the smoking. "I can talk to it here."

She is leaning against the doorframe and I assume she is speaking to me but I can't see her eyes due to deep shadows. "If my back hurts I can come in here and reassure myself it isn't a tumor. If I am bloated I can see clearly that I don't have ovarian cancer. My lungs are pinkish and my vessels large and open. My boy has been fixed, repaired with nylon and carbon based space age filaments. I can see this. I have evidence that he will be fine and normal and whole."

"Do we still say "space age"?" I ask. "I think this is an outdated phrase. When I think of the "space age" I envision guys with thick rimmed glasses and short sleeve dress shirts and plaid ties. I think of Tang and Teflon and command line computer interfaces. I think of giant rockets and balls of flame. We are in a time several steps past the "space" age. What do we call it? The "internet age"? That seems too fragile and speaks of Facebook and Flickr and Nigerian scams and emails promising penile enlargement and PORN, PORN PORN. I don't think this name has the gravitas we are looking for."

"Space Age 2.0" Laura offers.

"I like it" I say. "But I feel like this conveys something that I have to interact with. I want my technology to be passive yet strong, quiet yet indestructible, tiny yet capable of withstanding tremendous force, perfected on the micro rather than macro level, perfect down to the molecules and chemical bonds. And with cool pictures. It should have cool pictures so I can understand it without the mess and trouble of actual words."

"The Image Age" says Laura as she leans in to get a hug, never looking at me, staring only at her own unseeing eyes leering back at her from a picture on the desk.

THE DINNER PARTY

He inhaled deeply, feeling the air press against his ribs. Then blew it all out, forcefully but with patience, imagining a delicious stream of smoke exiting his mouth. He exhaled until he became lightheaded. Then he repeated the process. His eyes were sometimes open and sometimes closed. When open, they focused on the ceiling, its alternating patterns of shadow as the dawn light filtered into the bedroom. Not really light yet. Just that dawn hint of color. He continued breathing, his personal meditation. He tried to clear the thoughts that refused to leave.

She lay there next to him, curled up and aggressively over the center line. Limbs all akimbo. Her face serene. Blonde streaks randomly covered what he now saw as her almost smug expression. The air from her lips would stir the hair. Just a little. She snored. Not the room clearing blasts of the morbidly obese but the wheezy tightness of a deviated septum. A mouth breather she was.

His morning erection was alive if not fully realized. Like an old friend. He looked at it, wanting it to go away. He continued his breathing. Ellie seemed to be creeping closer. Not visibly perceptible but he knew she could sense his early morning weakness.

She moved like continental drift. Like a theory. She was one place then another without having seemed to traverse the area in between. When she moved the fault lines pressed against each other. Tremors resulted. On a rare occasion it was an earthquake. The shelves shook and glasses broke and adrenaline pumped through every cell. It was the earthquakes and maybe even the tremors that gave Ellie hope. That made Alvin ashamed. That tenuously held their marriage together.

Alvin got out of bed an instant before she touched him. His rising woke her, briefly. Ellie looked up sleepily and half smiled a good morning. Alvin forced a look that he thought was pleasant and hurried to the bathroom.

The bathroom to which he fled was his and his alone. They each had one. The monograms of their marriage should have hung over the frames of these doors rather than the towel rack. He approached the toilet and lifted the back cover. He fished out a ziplock bag containing two packs of cigarettes and a Bic. He shook the moisture from the package and pulled his precious bounty from the bag. The cigarette was lit in the same motion that the fan was turned on and a small outside window was opened. He resumed his breathing exercises but this time the air had a little punch. He held the counter due to lightheadedness and pictured himself floating away. Surrounded by nothing but space and quiet.

The nicotine brought on the usual urges and he dispensed with them casually - in the measured manner of the male of the species. He did not have a morning paper or a cup of coffee so things were not optimum. Perhaps he should put a coffee maker in his little room. That would certainly improve things. He always had something to read.

His library was impressive. The latest New Yorker, Sports Illustrated, two cookbooks, his latest crime novel, and several Victoria's Secret catalogues. As well, there was his pride and joy, a rather decent novel by a rather decent novelist. Though the novelist himself probably would be less than pleased with this particular display.

Wallace Stegner was the writer. Angle of Repose was the novel. Alvin read the entire book in three to four page intervals during his senior year in college. He liked the book. He really did. But it was the title and its place in the bathroom to which he was really attached.

He glanced at it now, thinking about the point of the work more than its humorous juxtaposition. The idea of the novel, or rather the meaning of its title, was, he thought, of rocks rolling down an irregularly sloped hill. Each stone finds a final resting place due to its individual circumstances, its velocity, its mass, its resistance and hardness. It looked back at the journey of one man and how he had come to his final resting place, filled with more than a little bitterness and resentment. But he left himself there, in that uncomfortable place, the place he came to rest. He stayed there, in his angle of repose, until inertia became impenetrable. He became a rock with roots.

In these moments Alvin would think about roots. Ponder them from his angle of repose. Their role as an organic form, life giving and essential. But he wasn't a plant and his roots were not deep, at least not yet. But they were growing just the same. Inevitably. His life was becoming intertwined with hers, financially, socially, and in uncountable less defined ways. He wanted someone to shove him. To start him rolling down the hill again. A man needs more than one resting place.

The shower was a delicious hiding place. The steam opened him and allowed his breathing to resume. He scrubbed himself clean and bathed in the comfort of the water. The shower was deaf to the world. The phone was not heard. Neither were voices or shouts. When he played it right, his mind was silent as well. What could be better than complete and utter silence?

His morning ritual was drawing to a close. He shaved and dried, not in that order. He combed his thinned hair and slapped some aftershave about. He left the sanctity of this room with a towel around his waist and his face stinging with contempt.

His closet was tired but quite decent. He dressed quickly and creatively, sensing colors and combinations, feeling the line and cut of his clothes, becoming himself, expanding as he became more confident. Alvin was very much attached to his wardrobe.

He sat on the edge of the bed to don his socks. He kept telling himself to bring a chair into the bedroom to give him some place to sit while he accomplished this very task. But he hadn't yet. So he sat on the bed and pulled up his dark, thin socks. He wiggled his toes and slid on his wingtips.

Ellie awakened at his activity. She pawed at him in her own imitation of the male morning erection. Unconscious and groping. Biological more than personal. It was that sort of grasp and that sort of reach. Alvin shrank from it and Ellie resumed her slumber.

He tightened the knot on his tie and began his exit. He paused at the foot of the bed, fighting at first the thought that was intruding upon him, the same thought he had every single morning. Every single one. Should he kill her and if so how could he get away with it?

How easy it would be. The strangling. The pummeling. The prosecution being the obvious problem. But it is the simple and illogical thought that spurs the logical mind. That flash of murder passing the mind's eye and the adrenaline surge that accompanied it, they were intoxicating in their vulgarity but he couldn't help himself from mentally exploring them again and again. The first time had been six years before, less than a year after their marriage, and he had hated himself for weeks afterward. But that feeling soon passed and the details of accomplishing this end became welcome intruders in his head. The thoughts started a cascade in his brain. Rolling inevitably downhill.

The reality of it all struck him only recently but the years of casual contemplation made it possible for his mind to accept the possibility, to not immediately dismiss them as silly or evil or as mere fantasy. The idea had somehow found a home in his brain, solidified itself in a mass of axons and neurotransmitters. It became actionable thought.

Alvin imagined what the reaction's of people to his internal life would be. The hatreds and instant judgements. Short shrift amateur psychological profiles that ignored his intelligence and depth, that refused to accept that the behavior of humans remained a mystery, that at times it was tangential and other times circumferential, that linear logic had no place in the examination of thought and behavior, that even given exact context people's actions remained largely unexplainable and in fact were belittled by attempts to do so.

Ellie's voice chirped from the bed an instant before he closed the bedroom door. "Everyone will be here at eight", she mumbled, her face buried in her pillow.

Alvin's mind shuttled and shifted. There was definitely something he should be remembering. Best to keep moving at such times and he walked out the front door and started his Toyota. It came to him, interrupting his early morning pleasure in getting out of the house. Just as Ellie planned it, thought Alvin. The dinner party. The fucking dinner party.

For Alvin, breakfast used to be the rushed inhalation of everything present, grabbing a coat and rushing out the door, desperate to avoid a lack of punctuality. But now Alvin was able to enjoy the morning meal at a casual, almost leisurely pace. He always fled the house at least an hour earlier than necessary. He left early to spend time with the newspaper and various processed pork products. They were his friends.

The counter at which he sat was not especially clean but then again it had plenty of ashtrays. Alvin smoked and ate biscuits covered in so much gravy he needed a fork and nibbled on sausage with a side of bacon. He peered into his own future and saw a man with a nitroglycerin tablet always at the ready.

The newspaper had a different personality depending on the day of the week. Alvin supposed this was self evident but he hadn't noticed it until he got married. The Friday paper, which he was now reading, tended towards the chunky and bloated side, filled with weekend previews and restaurant reviews and in depth sports. He loved the Friday paper. It was his favorite. It was friendly and informative yet not depressing and cloying as the Sunday paper seemed to be. To Alvin, the Sunday edition was a little too desperate to be loved.

He perused the local news section for exotic homicides or drunk driving arrests of friends before moving on to his favorite section. A listing of marriage licenses applied for, divorces filed, and divorces granted filled a three inch space each day. He was always amazed at the number in each category. The divorces seemed to far outweigh the marriages and it seemed to him the entire city should soon be single. He always knew at least one couple and somehow this knowledge comforted him. It connected him to the inner lives of others while, at the same time, giving the vicarious thrill of peeping uninvited into the lives of his neighbors. He knew something he shouldn't.

Work was quiet when he arrived but there were stirrings of activity. The five secretaries employed by his firm were beginning to file and collate and bitch about their spouses. The cute and single one, Amy, would probably still be several more minutes in arriving.

Alvin felt slightly more alive, more real, with each step into the office. He smiled broadly and chatted casually, throwing out silly jokes and seeing himself as extremely amusing. He liked himself at work and this troubled him greatly.

He felt his work persona was the real him, alive, witty, happy, competent. But more and more often it seemed to him that this was just his act, that the real him was the irritable, pessimistic, grumpy man he was at home. It angered him that Ellie had this same knowledge, that she had seen behind his curtain and knew him to be the schmuck that he was. She knew he was neither sure of himself nor in control. She robbed him of the man he wanted to be.

The leather chair in his office was cold to the touch but inviting just the same. He ran a finger across his desk and smiled at his reflection in its shiny surface. The office itself was small and piss poor, the office of an associate of uncertain promise at a small firm in a mid - size city. His law school diploma hung in its elaborate frame on the wall behind him. A picture of Ellie was on his desk, it was six years old and he had grown tired of it. She was smiling her false smile, all pearly white teeth and slightly cocked head. He had better pictures of her, most notably a series of lingerie shots she had taken a year earlier to spice up Christmas. He often wanted to put one of those on his desk, preferably the one with the cowboy hat.

He pulled a file from his desk and scribbled notes. He made phone calls, altering his personality for each in an attempt to achieve his desired goals. He dictated and drafted. He did all this with a smooth calm and a sense of undeniable purpose.

At lunch he ate a corned beef sandwich with a too sour pickle and joked with the secretaries. They told bawdy stories and shared tidbits of gossip, juicy and baseless. They laughed about impotent husbands and absent boyfriends. He flirted with the always sexy Amy, wishing he were single.

His mental faithlessness used to bother him but it didn't anymore. He figured he was one of the good ones. Sinning only in thought, never in deed. Ellie was lucky to have him.

The afternoon was much like the morning but shorter. The world anticipates the weekend and his firm had a policy of casual Fridays that included the option to wear jeans and, unless a specific case required work, all staff were allowed to go home at two p.m. Alvin looked for ways to delay his departure but the fact was he simply wasn't all that busy and he eventually gave up and left the office around three.

The streets were crowded and, to Alvin, seemed festive. He was jealous of the city's mood and the apparent joy of it inhabitants. He just drove for several miles, the radio off and his thoughts an incoherent screech. He began to calm as the drive continued. He skirted the perimeter of the city, driving without stops on the interstate bypass. He was soothed by the rhythms of driving and the familiar sights of his hometown.

The road was not a lonely place. It was filled with cars and faces that had attitudes and personalities. It had businesses and scenery which called to mind memories of when these things were different. Alvin drove and played with the emptiness in his mind, singing along with songs on the radio now, unsure how he knew the words. The road filled him with emotion rather than thought, undirected and vague. This is what he needed. This is what he liked. Constant changes in his reality. Changes so swift he could not analyze them, they simply flowed over him. He drove and he sang and he watched and he shifted. He smiled as well.

His roundabout journey brought him to a specialty shop. He picked up meat and bread and spices and paid a ridiculous price for it all. He was surrounded by many others doing the same. He, as well as they, were quite pleased with themselves for their taste and their style.

Homeward bound, he thought. Bound to home. He arrived and just sat in his driveway for about five minutes, decompressing. He rubbed the head of his sad Basset Hound and unpacked his groceries. He tried to run through a mental list of the evening's menu and the timing involved in preparing each item. His mind kept wandering and finally he gave up.

In the first place he hated dinner parties. They were always going to one or giving one. The same couples were always involved. This had become their social life and he wasn't crazy about it. It seemed to him a big game of one upsmanship in the wines or the cuisine. Competitiveness as to who was the wittiest conversationalist.

In the second place, the fact that the participants were always the same had led to the chronic problems of all long term friendships. Unseen alliances developed and quiet hatreds passed unspoken between individuals like invisible motion detectors. False alarms were constantly set off.

Dinner parties involved couples and couples were not friends. Individuals were friends and their spouses came along out of social necessity. So one of Alvin's buddies would bring his second wife who Ellie hated or Ellie would invite a male friend from work she adored and Alvin very much wanted to strike. God forbid if Alvin had a female friend. Ellie would be catty and the invited friend's husband would be jealous. But everyone would smile and compliment the food and the decor.

His final problem was that all his murder fantasies involved dinner parties. Ellie's murder that was, but incidental casualties would be well tolerated, maybe even encouraged.

How do you kill your wife? Alvin had given the matter more than a little thought. All the intricate plots and schemes in the world were useless. The husband is always the one and only suspect. Alvin decided there were only two ways to kill a wife.

The first is to hire somebody, have them abduct or rob you in front of witnesses, and have them kill her in the process. This is an excellent method but requires being significantly wounded yourself in order to make the set up look good. Worse it involves hiring thugs and it is a certainty that at some point in the future they would trade information about their role in the scheme to avoid jail time on some other charge.

The second, and best way is to kill her in front of witnesses and make it look accidental. This is simple, involves few lies, no money, minimal investigation, and its all over in the blink of an eye. He just had to make it a good accident.

Alvin practiced strange things, thing actually. A family gun had been purchased two years earlier, at the insistence of Ellie after a spate of home invasions in the neighborhood. Alvin was initially reluctant due to a hatred of guns but the purchase was made and Alvin became a gun owner. He went to the shooting range for awhile. He was an alright shot but lacked motivation. He began venturing to the woods outside of town, firing at trees and squirrels, doing a quick draw. Then he became more focused. He practiced shooting with the gun crossways in his lap, firing the gun by accidentally brushing his finger across the trigger.

Alvin heard a key in the door and rapidly feigned sleep. He was stretched out on the couch, his head cocked at an unnatural angle. He produced a touch of drool and let it trickle down his cheek. Ellie entered loudly, allowing the weight and the detritus of a long day fall from her person. Keys and coat and purse clattered to the floor. Alvin's mock slumber continued.

Ellie came in the den and observed her husband. She sat on the couch arm, near his head, and looked at his face. She often had difficulty figuring that face out, deciphering the thoughts behind the smile. She liked the face most when it slept, when it was childlike and guileless. She watched the movements of his chest, feeling an attachment to them, as if she somehow owned them. She tried to match his respiratory rate with her own. She wanted to kiss him but didn't. She shook him awake instead.

Alvin faked a good startle and muttered some unintelligible hellos. Ellie scooted under him and placed his head on her lap. Her linen skirt was wrinkled but smooth to the touch. He was turned on for a moment, but then she spoke and it passed. Why did they have to speak?

"They're supposed to be here at eight. Did you get the wine?" She sounded exhausted as she asked.

He shook his head no and curled up, feeling a very real tiredness of his own, an all over malaise. "I got all the food though. Shouldn't they bring the wine?"

She stroked his hair and he felt her sharp nails on his scalp, the sound conducting through his skull and echoing loudly in his ears. "Of course they'll bring wine but we need a couple of bottles too." She said it as if she were speaking to a child. Unspoken was the fact that it must be better than anything they would bring over. Failing that it should be odd or interesting or at the very least more expensive.

"I'll go grab something in an hour or two." He wanted to send her. Let her founder on the shores of wine selection. Unfortunately she would probably do fine and spend way too much money. Smile and bat her eyes and ask the liquor store owner for his suggestions. She was a smiler and batterer of eyes as well as a mouth breather.

What Alvin wanted was a nap and a drink, maybe in that order and maybe not. He couldn't sleep so a drink was his only choice. He rose and poured himself a bourbon rocks. He glanced about and absorbed what had become of their home in the last six years. It was a constant state of flux, a stylistic nightmare if truth be told. Alvin was a minimalist at heart and their was nothing minimal about their house.

Ellie's taste in home decor was dictated by a drunken lesbian who's sole interest seemed to be a whopping commission though Alvin suspected bedding Ellie was also on her list, an idea which Alvin didn't completely oppose. She fed Ellie's ego and her ego needed feeding. The cost of the furniture was nearing the cost of the home and there was no end in site. Pieces were constantly being changed out or upgraded. He was forbidden to even touch the vast majority of the items. Alvin's only responsibility was the bar and this was always embarrassingly well stocked.

Ellie looked at him disapprovingly as he sat down with his drink. Sometimes her approval mattered and sometimes it didn't. He wasn't sure how he felt on that day. Nauseous maybe.

The bourbon was cold and tasteless, causing a slight gag on the way down. He fiddled with the clicker but good television was hard to find. Everything seemed forced and overdone. He thought maybe this was because he was trying to find something good enough to please Ellie, to entertain them both at the same time. Something good enough to be engrossing so that each second of interpersonal silence didn't tick loudly in his brain.

He found nothing. The silence remained unbridged. He had a second drink and it went down easier this time. He needed to pace himself, he thought. The tension of the silence mounted but he wouldn't be the first to crack. Ellie began to cry and scurried off to the bedroom.

She looked at herself in the mirror. Her eyes were a little streaked. She saw the creases and the lines but they were not her focus. What she saw was a blur. Anger morphing into sadness. She was tired of her emotion being yanked about, at his whim, depending on his ever changing moods. Some days she felt a failure. More often she was just mad. Mad at his awkward inattention and his equally awkward affection. She felt life should be a much smoother and simpler ride. She thought that perhaps she was too sensitive.

She decided to lie down and soon was asleep. Her dreams were unclear and distinctly unpleasant. She woke suddenly, staring at her hands. She hated her damn hands. There were no aerobics for them. They showed age like a horse's teeth. She began to bite a nail but stopped, moved to the little alcove that was their bedroom window. She fished in her purse for a Virginia Slim, or a Vagina Slime as her high school boyfriend used to call them. She huddled in the alcove and blew smoke out the window, her knees pulled tightly to her chest. She studied her hands and the end of the cigarette. She looked at their yard and at their driveway, their cars. The personalities of the cars were intimately intertwined with the person that drove them. His messy and dusty Toyota. Her immaculate but dented Lexus, the luxury car they couldn't afford to get fixed.

As she sat she moved through the rooms of her mind. Not long ago Alvin had been in all of them, a presence if not an importance. He defined the parameters of her thoughts and her feelings. But over the last year she had tidied up, swept the dust and cleared the cobwebs, maybe even cracked a window. Alvin was now in just a few rooms though his scent inhabited them all. He lingered just a bit but that's all it was, lingering. She didn't want to be in one of those rooms with him now, but she had to be, at least in one of them.

Alvin concentrated on not concentrating. He took his basset, Legs, out for a walk. It was like dragging an anchor behind him. Legs wasn't much of a walker, or a hunter, or a trickster, or a snuggler. He was more or less a plasma lump with ears. But walks with the dog were one of a dozen excuses he used to get out of the house. He would go to the store three or four times a day, run errands at all hours. Originally these had just

been excuses to smoke but more and more they became reasons to simply leave the house.

He wandered his neighborhood. The fall air was cool and the sun seemed anxious to go to bed for the evening, tired of constantly putting on a bright and shining face. The streets of this area were fresh asphalt and wound confusingly into numerous cul-de-sacs, a slight grade to them all. The houses were smallish but multi - leveled and new, all painted various shades of white. The yards were small and neat, many with for sale or sold signs. There was a lot of turnover in the area.

There were people outside besides him, couples that reminded him of Ellie and himself. Hell, they were Ellie and himself. White bread clones sent from some distant planet to quietly populate suburbia. They were all very interchangeable. He fantasized sometimes about pulling a switch, conspiring with one of his male neighbors, drugging their wives and dumping them in wheelbarrows for a midnight swap, at long last a slight change in tastes and aromas but at the same time no real difference. Maybe he would trade for a woman that could give decent head. Alvin then thought better. No man would trade a wife that gave decent head.

The effort of dragging the dog around the neighborhood became too much. He returned to his home and sat in the driveway, smoking and flaunting his untamed habit for the world to see. Legs looked up at him with those sad and stoned eyes, bloodshot and round. Alvin nodded at him, sensing an emotional companion.

Eventually he screwed up his courage and went back inside. He could hear water running upstairs. It was soothing and rhythmic, cleansing waters that signified mornings in and evenings out, washing off the past and the stench of the day gone by. It was starting over again, collecting all new dirt and smells.

Alvin went to the stereo and filled the room with Van Morrison, a shower to the ears and mind. He set about preparing dinner, a task at which he felt satisfyingly at home.

He seasoned the meat and heated the pans. He chopped and diced and measured and sorted. The aromas filled the air and he could taste them on his tongue and in his nose. It made him a little giddy. He danced and sang along to the music and poured a bourbon for himself. He sipped it first then threw it back, the music again striking him, sensing for a moment the calm pace and melody. His eyes closed, the world was entirely new, a place of exploration and experience, happy and inviting, an arena of possibility. He felt Ellie's arms around his waist and the trance was broken.

His mood was not completely destroyed. Ellie was wearing a terry cloth robe with a towel wrapped loosely around her head. Her skin looked shiny and new from the fresh scrubbing it had just received. Her green eyes looked lively and expressive. To Alvin she looked sixteen years old.

She felt sixteen years old, watching silently as he moved. He was so graceful and in control in the kitchen. There are senses of things that are not necessarily primal but are the basis of original attraction. Ellie had a flashback watching Alvin dance in the kitchen, watching the way he moved, the relation of his shoulders to his waist. That was it. He had a grace and economy of movement that men most often lacked, nothing unnecessary . So that when he moved it had intent and was special. She knew it had a purpose. She had always been so kinetic and lost that she reveled in someone who seemed to have tamed their movement. She liked that he danced by himself.

Alvin took her face in his hands and kissed her, soft at first but then with growing urgency.

"Ew. Bourbon and smoke. That's disgusting." But she smiled when she said it. Smiled at the affection if not the act itself. "When did you start smoking again?"

There was no joy in life, thought Alvin. The simplest of moments, a second of pleasure, turned into criticism. He rallied anyway. "The drink made me want one."

"You must have had a pack with you to want one."

Alvin conceded defeat. The smoking conversation always ended sounding like it was more about infidelity than a bad habit. But for the moment he still liked her. She smelled of soap. He liked soap and he liked bathrobes. He kissed her again and slid a hand into the slit in her robe, tugging lightly on the sash. He fondled her briefly, the flash of excitement making him feel juvenile and puerile. He could sense a reciprocation, both of them giving some thought to tearing one off on the floor. Then they both thought better of it. Ellie pulled away slowly, as if trying not to offend.

"So what are we having?"

"You'll know soon enough." He grinned at her a bit, almost a leer. "I have to go get the wine. Can you watch the stove?"

A look of sheer terror crossed her face. All blood rushed to her extremities. It appeared for a moment that she would swoon but she pulled it together at the last second. She tried to say something but an unintelligible stammer is all that she produced.

He laughed at her. "I'll just turn everything off until I get home." Ellie still appeared to be shaken but she nodded her approval of the plan.

He was back in the car. He had made it out yet again, smoking freely and feeling more than a little buzzed. It was becoming darker and colder and maybe the wind was blowing a little harder.

He could have gone to a liquor store two minutes from his house. Instead he ventured further under the pretense of quality. A more distant journey held far greater rewards. He could smoke two cigarettes each way.

He milled around the store, eyeing the wines and feeling his usual low level frustration. There were no bargains that he could see. He ended up with an overpriced Merlot, a wine like his wife, a blend. A wine whose asset is its immediacy. It has minimal staying power and questionable improvement with age. Christ, he thought to himself, I married a California red.

Before he left the store he grabbed a bottle of scotch and a bottle of gin as well, on the off chance the evening might turn ugly. He mentally checked off the drinks and briefly scrolled through the appetizer, the soup, the salad, and the entree, imagining how they would look on presentation.

His distance from home seemed greater than it had on the original trip. The thought of driving right on by his house seemed attractive, to just keep going into the limitless beyond, or at least to the nearest bar. He had this feeling often and fought it daily. It was interesting to him that it most often occurred while traveling towards home, almost never on the trip away. Maybe the act of driving by the house was important. He didn't know. Most of the time he didn't care.

Ellie was drinking sherry when he returned. This was an odd habit of hers that Alvin would never understand. She could drink sherry all night, get downright loopy on the too sweet stuff. Just the smell of it made Alvin queasy. Ellie was reading one of her books as she drank. She was a voracious reader of mind numbing crap, mostly mysteries. She read one a day on the average, like a vitamin.

He liked that she read. It was hours a day that he did not need to make conversation. Which is what it was all about, he had decided, minimizing the uncomfortable moments, the awkward silences. Books, tv, and the all important movie rental nights combined to almost eliminate the need for conversation altogether and provided topics to bridge the moments when talk was all they had.

He turned the oven on and continued dinner preparations. He settled things so he could go upstairs and shower. The steps creaked under his feet. Ellie didn't look up from her book as her husband passed.

He stripped in the bathroom and saw himself in the mirror, appearing much older than he felt he should. He did not look muscular and he did not look sinewy. He looked a little flaccid. He looked very, very pale. He felt his hair still looked pretty passable. He climbed into the steamy water and turned off the world.

Ellie kept reading, thoughts flying through her head at an astounding rate. She heard the shower and moved outside to the porch, bringing her book and her sherry along. She lit up a smoke and sucked hard. It felt clean and clear, mixing well with her drink. The book she was reading wasn't very interesting. Her books rarely were. She liked them like this, more like mind candy than any attempt at self improvement. She felt a sudden distaste for Alvin. She knew this would soon pass. It always did. But sometimes he just seemed so limp, so impotent, so clueless, as if he were some kind of strange ghost. He smiled and talked but he seemed to function at a level barely above the brainstem. Often she had a nearly uncontrollable urge to slap him.

The sherry tasted thick and sweet, intoxicating on multiple levels. She lit a second cigarette and inhaled deeply, careful not to smear her lipstick. She stared at her fingernails. They seemed long and smooth. Her secret was using formaldehyde on them which she thought gave them strength. She clicked them against each other, liking the soft sound they made. She thought for a moment that she was well equipped for a serious cocaine habit. She could go two fisted. Another career opportunity missed.

It was late dusk and the cars driving by had their headlights turned on. Ellie always felt blind at this time of day. The flat light didn't penetrate well and gave objects soft borders that seemed to flow in an almost hallucinatory way. She had to squint to see anything.

The children playing in their assorted yards appeared to her as grotesque gnomes, confirming her feelings about children of all sorts. A basketball rolled into the street and one of the spawn of middle earth scrambled after it. A car became visible in the distance and barreled down the road towards the child. She did not call out though the child was possibly within earshot. She just watched. She wondered if they would collide.

They didn't. The driver slowed carefully, showing all due caution. The child looked up and smiled. The responsible motor vehicle operator wagged a finger at the careless imp. The youngster shrugged his shoulders and laughed and the driver laughed as well. Ellie felt vaguely pissed. She got up and went back in the house, leaving two spent butts in the yard. This is what sucks about life in the burbs, she thought. There was no slaughter in the streets.

Alvin dressed carefully and well. Wool slacks with a white cotton shirt buttoned to the top provided the start. To this he added a dark olive vest and a lighter olive blazer. He looked at himself in the mirror and for the first time since arriving home felt smugly satisfied. He thought for a moment about why he was spending so much time getting dressed, about who it was he was trying to impress. He wasn't sure. He'd think more about it later.

In moments he was back at work with his pots and pans and everything was progressing nicely. He wore an apron and thought himself quite chic for doing so. His jacket was off and his sleeves rolled up. He strained the soup and transferred some potatoes, cooking them in the milk and cream soup. It was flavored with onions and garlic and shallots. He tossed some canned clams along with their juice into the pot and pureed the whole deal with a hand mixer. The soup thickened and he stuck a finger in to taste it deciding it needed some salt and he added some white pepper as well. He checked again for thickness, adding a teaspoon of flour slowly as he stirred. He took the pot off the heat and set it aside.

The doorbell rang, an invasion even more egregious than the infernal telephone. He hated their bell. It donged three times in a sing song manner. He thought to himself how superior a good solid knock was to any doorbell. It was easier to ignore a knock, like blowing off a salesman or a girl scout. But a doorbell was powerful, undeniable. It carried with it a message. The people are coming, the people are coming.

The particular people were Brad and Nancy, two people that shouldn't have married for the simple reason that their names sounded grating when pronounced together. Brad and Nancy. Nancy and Brad.

Brad was Ellie's wildly effeminate co - worker. He was her office manager. He took care of personnel matters and solved interoffice disputes. He also got on Alvin's last nerve. Alvin pictured him bouncing around the water cooler clad in suspenders and tassled loafers, gesticulating wildly as he gossiped and told humorous tales. Alvin felt Brad should get a memo. It would read simply, "You're gay. Deal with it."

Also not dealing with it was Brad's fairly corpulent wife. She was nice enough in a too earnest type of way. She was a perennial student, currently working on a master's in Art History. She dressed in Lane Bryant and seemed to be always smiling. She liked sports and drank bourbon. Alvin felt more comfortable around her than her husband.

"Hey honey," Brad said to Elllie. "Damn, what smells so good. The chef hard at it in there? Man this place looks great. It looks better every time we come. You have to give me that decorator's number. Oooh, the bookshelves are terrific. They match the couch perfectly. Ooh that smells good."

They giggled and whispered together, huddling out of Alvin's earshot. The doorbell rang again and Annette and Ted Mange made their appearance. That was their name, or at least it was his name and she sadly had acquired it. The disease of the same designation possibly afflicted them both, him more severely than her.

Ted's hair just skirted the outside of his head, like it was afraid of direct sunlight. His dome was well polished and shone brightly beneath the flourescent lights. To his credit he did nothing to conceal his baldness. He did spend a lot of time rubbing it. Like an autoerotic movement it was something that seemed to give him pleasure.

Annette was also balding, but of course noone would mention it. It was mostly on top. Her hair was always poofy and curled in an attempt to conceal the bare patches. It was colored auburn but the unnatural auburn of a mediocre dye job. He figure was rock solid but a thickish mustache limited her attractiveness. Alvin often wondered if she used steroids.

Ted popped his head in the kitchen. He was wearing jeans and a tie. He was very short and his stature gave him an impish charm. He shook Alvin's hand vigorously, making a slight tilting movement of his head towards Brad. Alvin shrugged his shoulders and continued cooking as the final couple arrived. Ted pulled a Bass out of the fridge and put a French Cabernet on the counter.

William and Jilly entered and it suddenly occurred to Alvin why he had taken such care with his appearance. Not only was her name Jilly but she expected people to call her that. At the last dinner party she had produced her birth certificate to document the reality of the appellation. It also documented her age, twenty - one. Twenty fucking one, thought Alvin as he watched Jilly bounce down the hallway. Just saying it made him angry.

Her hair was black and long and perfectly straight. Her skin was ghostly pale and set off her eyes which were huge and brown. The face was flattish but unique and it had grown on Alvin. She was tallish and fairly slim, flat chested with a nicely rounded ass. She exuded a youthful confidence and this showed in her bouncy gait. Every step pissed Ellie off. She was a second wife.

William was Alvin's best friend. He was short and a little rumpled. He seemed to smile constantly, maybe because he was working on making his third million at age thirty-five. The occupation that garnered such high rewards was vague. He had holdings in several small businesses. He was well informed. He had an office and a secretary. That's all anybody knew. That and the fact that his first wife died in a car accident. Alvin envied him that.

William brought two bottles into the kitchen, a red and a white. He winked at Alvin and Alvin felt comfortable for a minute, sensing an ally, forgetting for the moment that he wanted to defile his best friend's child bride. Such were the problems of Alvin's adulthood.

Alvin pulled his appetizer out of the oven, two phyllo dough pizzas. They had a thin, crisp crust, a layer of cream cheese, thinly sliced tomatoes, mushrooms, and a scattering of peppers with parmesan and mozzarella on top. He delivered the food to the huddled and chattering group in the living room and hurriedly moved back to the solitude of the kitchen.

Alvin kept an eye on the gathering through the kitchen portal. They were talking about the admittedly sorry state of local schools, with some slight digressions into Annette's rather interesting hair. Ellie was playing bartender and doing quite well at it. William came into the kitchen carrying a martini.

"So what's the word dear chef?", William asked.

"She's dead", William responded.

"Ellie? She looks quite fetching for a corpse."

"Shut up Bill. How can I talk to you? You're walking around with the Seventeen cover girl."

"Talk to me as you would a god."

"That's what I'm afraid of. That I'll spend my life trying to be decent and then I'll die and God will be some small Italian cheese with a teenage wife."

"It's a distinct possibility. But I'm not Italian. I'm adopted."

"You're not God either."

"Perhaps."

They stood in silence, Alvin tasting his martini. He referred to it as a clear drink with a dark taste. Ted joined them, drinking scotch.

"Is this the meeting place?"

"For the moment."

"What's on the stove?"

"Lamb chops."

"Curry?"

"Mint."

They fell into a lengthy discussion of local butchers and their comparative quality and selection. This led to herbs and seasonings, cookware and presentation, grades of meat, the order of the menu, vegetables. All very manly.

This always struck Alvin as odd but he had come to accept it. Women in the nineties just didn't cook, and when they did it was a fearful experience. So the men had taken up the banner. Not so much proudly but more in a continuing quest for quality. In an ideal world good food would just materialize, perfect and finished. But if they left these women alone in the biodome the water with them could live comfortably knowing it would never be boiled. If it wasn't a salad they were not interested. They didn't eat, they grazed. So the men learned.

Each of the men, including Brad, could lay out a respectable spread. Quietly they shared recipes and each would admit, albeit under his breath, that he was a regular viewer of more than one cooking show.

As the three men talked and laughed in the kitchen Alvin slowly slid outside himself. He pictured each person at the party doing the same, each person with a spiritual doppelganger giving voice to true and honest thought, critiquing their physical selves with arms crossed and heads tilted in a posture of extreme arrogance.

Alvin's critique involved the sad aging of the trio. Faces lacked firmness. Fleshy jaws and bellies were concealed as neatly as possible beneath well tailored costumes. Their conversations were barely coherent and nearly banal. They tried to discuss things of import and depth but their eyes were incapable of turning inward, at least incapable of doing so with any clarity or depth of vision and once the inward looking eye managed to focus its frame of reference was so skewed that the viewer had lost focus on the world around him.

They all moved to the den. A small blaze was flickering in the rarely used fireplace. Alvin sat on the floor, legs crossed indian style. He was conscious of the fact that this was wrinkling his slacks but he ignored this for the moment and sipped on his drink. The group was divided neatly into couples, each twosome engaging in conversation as a single entity, the discussions themselves dependent on the two couples involved. Alvin / Ellie found themselves mumbling with Nancy / Brad about workplace trivia, various players and personages in their professional lives, an evil tramp, a grumpy boss, the unbelievable lack of intelligence and competence in all of their superiors.

Ellie liked this part of the evening. She looked at the group as she would a painting or a photograph. Everything was in it's place. She was satisfied with the composition of the image. She was most pleased with Alvin. He blended well at these events. He was handsome and well groomed. He moved easily and had a sweet and charming smile, not overdone, very genuine. His teeth were shiny white but slightly out of line, the imperfection adding to his attractiveness. She wanted to touch him and after some hesitation did so. She leaned against him, gently, shoulder to shoulder, like they were on a first date and she wanted him to know she was interested. A slight shock of warmth spread through her when they touched, or maybe it was the fire, or maybe the booze. He talked in a quiet baritone and she closed her eyes for a moment, listening to the cadence of his speech. In many ways she had internalized that voice. It had become the voice of her inner thoughts. The one that spoke to her in approving tones.

They each had a second drink and the pizzas were finished. Alvin cleared the plates and went into the kitchen to finish up dinner. Ellie followed. Alvin was tearing leaves of arugala and iceberg lettuce, placing them in a large wooden bowl. Ellie slipped a hand around his waist.

"Is there anything I can do to help?"

Alvin was shocked at the offer as well as the affection. "Sure, I need some dressing." He began chopping tomatoes and cucumbers.

Ellie looked unsure. Slowly she moved to the refrigerator and opened the door, searching its innards for a bottle she could recognize. "I don't see any."

"Just make some real quick."

Ellie just looked at him, confused, as if he had suggested alchemy. "Forget it. It will just take me a minute. Get everybody to the table." Ellie smiled at this assignment and walked away.

Ted's bald head popped around the corner. "Can I help?"

"Sure. Make up a dressing."

Ted scoped the fridge and pulled out some dijon and some mayo. He found a bowl and put a spoonful of the mustard and half as much mayo into it and mixed those with some olive oil and vinegar. He added a dash of pepper and whipped it vigorously. Alvin slid the salad bowl over and Ted poured the dressing over its contents. Alvin tossed and mixed.

The salad was served and the first bottle of wine was uncorked. The group was subdivided differently now. Ellie and Alvin were on opposite ends of the table. All couples were separated, at least one person removed from their significant other in a semi random boy girl boy fashion, like a rhyming scheme. They all tasted their wine and fought with their salads which, Alvin had noticed, had leaves that were far too large to be easily handled. Live and learn, he thought. The dressing was perfect.

Jilly was sitting next to Alvin, on his right, his good side. He was very happy about this. Jilly wore a one piece cotton print dress. Little flowers dotted her nubbinish breasts. If he looked hard enough Alvin could sense a little cleavage and perhaps the outline of a nipple.

Her face was round, still possessing the firm baby fat of youth, not the angled fleshlessness of excessive dieting or the slight chubbiness of the aggressively bulemic. It was the beauty of youth, pure and simple. The beauty that pervades the Calvin Klein ads that make the viewer so uncomfortable. It was an irreplaceable and fleeting quality. Sometimes Alvin's need to possess it again was so powerful it made his chest hurt.

The salads were finished and Alvin cleared the table. He removed some heated bowls from the dishwasher and filled them with the creamy soup, sprinkling some parsley on top for color. He placed the entree in the oven to heat it up. The soup was served along with a second bottle of wine. The soup was light and flavorful if somewhat odd in texture. It served the function of the soup course, to create demand for the real meal. The conversation reflected this. They were all holding back any new stories or humorous anecdotes for the dinner conversation. It was all smiles and short statements for the soup.

Ellie was seated between Bill and Nancy. She liked Bill. Everybody liked Bill. And there was nothing not to like about Nancy. But Ellie was still unhappy with her seat. She could see that Alvin was fascinated with Jilly. It was bad enough that Bill walked around with a child like that. Alvin didn't have to encourage it.

She accepted the fact of it, the eternal male quest for youth. But she never understood it. People improved with age. She was sure of this. They grew and changed and could reflect back on mistakes and successes. What was life without a past? It seemed so shallow and meaningless. But perhaps she invested too much in her past, counting on it to provide the texture of her life. Maybe she was not interested enough in the present. Maybe people weren't reliable enough to base a life on a common past.

Her thoughts and feelings were so intertwined with Alvin that she simply could not separate them. Was it possible that he was different? That when he receded into his mind, spent the day in its shrouding mists and endless caverns, that he viewed himself alone. Saw himself not as a part of a couple but instead the couple as something external to him. It hurt her head to think about it.

The soup was finished and the bowls cleared. Alvin placed all the used dishes in the dishwasher, trying to save some later work. He pulled the lamb from the oven and cut it into servings. Each person would receive two chops with mint sauce sprinkled on top and spread about the sides. Scalloped potatoes in a cream and parmesan cheese sauce were added to each plate. A sprinkling of parsley and a sprig of rosemary were the final touches. He dropped some Pillsbury pastry dough in the oven, timing it to be ready on cue.

As soon as the plates were out Alvin realized there would not be enough food. The chops were small and he had none in reserve. He hoped the multiple courses and the heavy potatoes would be enough to satisfy. If that wasn't enough he figured the copious consumption of wine would blur everybody's critical faculties and memories of the meal.

Alvin enjoyed the main course. He always did. People became carnivores and this is how he liked them. Maybe they didn't realize how live and anatomic the meat had looked only hours before, but it seemed to him on some level they had to. They were eating flesh. Seared with heat and left slightly raw in the center. Chewing on barely dead tissue. The fat and connective fibers rounding out the flavor, giving it depth.

He watched Jilly chew, daintily and in small bites. Despite her petite frame and guileless eyes the fact that she was eating flesh remained. Her canines tore at the meat, shredding its edges. A slight reddish discoloration appeared on her pearly whites as the juices slid off of them. It was so base and medieval, all done with properly placed utensils and napkins in the lap. It made Alvin a little horny.

The main course took longer than the others, as it should. The conversations of the table became one instead of four small discussions. Bill related a rather long tale between bites and sips. It involved a group of extremely large women. How he became involved with these women was unclear and remained that way.

The gist of the story was this. Bill went over to the house of these four large women. He was inspecting a property or trying to purchase their land or some such thing. These large women were extremely large, well over three hundred pounds apiece. They lived in a small one story home that had a crumbling foundation and sagging porch. Bill thought these defects appropriate for the occupants. All wore huge, one piece mumus, their breasts and bellies extending forward to create the impression of a smooth anterior contour.

When he visited their abode they were seated around a smallish kitchen table, mysterious water stains visible and distracting on the walls and ceiling. The chairs were straining under their weight, the wood looking as if it might literally explode. Bill looked around and noticed that save the water stains the entire home seemed to lack color of any kind. The only exception being a dirty orange couch in the corner of the living room, its frayed fabric partially obscured by piles of newspapers. The women were sharing a large chocolate pie, eating meaty slivers with their fingers. Bill politely turned down a bite for himself.

A small man, a very small man, less than five feet, slowly emerged from beneath the stacks of papers on the couch where he had been sleeping. His eyes were wide and his face unshaven. He had a look of near catatonia. Bill asked the women who he was. They answered in unison that he was their boyfriend. Bill nodded understandingly, now recognizing the look on the grubby little man's face. It was fear.

Opal, the largest of the group and distinguished by her light blue mumu and sprouting goatee, suddenly doubled over with abdominal pain. She rolled on the floor like a turtle on its back, unable to right herself even if she wanted to.

"I'M GONNA TAKE A SHIT.", Opal screamed. "I'M GONNA TAKE A SHIT RIGHT HERE."

The roomful of faces turned to Bill, assuming that since he was wearing a suit and and polished wingtips that he was the closest thing present to a doctor. Bill wondered if even a real doctor would ever intervene in an act of defecation. He moved to the side of the woman who seemed the size of a small continent, feeling her tense abdomen. She screamed and lifted her knees off the ground, her legs in the lithotomy position.

Bill hated to look between those legs but he felt compelled. The second most disturbing thing he saw was her utter lack of underwear. Most disturbing was what appeared to be a blueish, smooth headed alien slowly emerging from Opal's vagina, along with a slithering brown load from her anus.

Over his shoulder Bill noted he had an audience of overweight women wanting an update.

"She is, in fact, taking a shit.", Bill reported.

Bill turned his attention back to the emerging alien, recognition finally coming to him. It was an expanding membrane and he stared at it, transfixed. He stared as it bulged and bulged then finally exploded, splashing fluid all over Bill and his Armani suit. Everyone in the room was screaming, including Bill and excepting the little man on the couch. He had seen much greater horrors.

As Bill wiped the putrid gunk from his eyes he saw a small head oozing from this enormous woman. He moved between her legs, proud of himself for his clarity of thought and firmness of stomach. Emma, the smallest of the ladies, had the emergency room on the phone and an ambulance was on the way.

The baby poured into Bill's outstretched hands like a milkshake from a soda fountain, blue and slimy and slippery. Emma said to tie the umbilical cord with a shoelace and put the baby on Opal's stomach. Bill did this, pulling the lace from his soiled three hundred dollar shoes. He tied a bow, like on a shoe. He found this funny because who would untie the knot? He released the crying child to his screaming mother and thought his work was done.

It was, for the moment. Opal continued to yell and push. Bill thought for a moment that she might be having twins. His fears seemed confirmed by what appeared to be a head emerging from the bloody orifice. It proved to be the placenta. It came out in a rush of blood and fluid. The odor was ripe.

Things then calmed and the child cried happily, a stalk swinging from his belly button like a hanging fern. The ambulance arrived and Bill buttoned his coat and walked out quietly, nodding to the small man in the corner as he left.

Dinner was done and everybody sipped wine and lingered at the table. The dishes were cleared a third time and Alvin placed some semi - sweet chocolate in a pan to melt. He watched it slowly turn liquid as he loaded the dishwasher well beyond capacity. He added sugar and cream and stirred well. The puffed pastries were done and split in half. He placed a dollop of vanilla ice cream on the bottom half of each then replaced the top, making little ice cream sandwiches. He poured the chocolate sauce over each and served the crispy confection slightly warm.

The desserts were eaten slowly, the crowd drunken by now. Everybody laughed easily as social restraint began to fade. Jilly gestured wildly while telling the story of a high school boyfriend and the back seat of his pick up. They all laughed at the near rape experience and its ending in sad impotence. Alvin watched Bill's face to see if the story bothered him. This was not a tale told from remote memory for Jilly. It was three years ago. But Bill seemed unperturbed, a model of maturity.

Dessert was over and people retired to the restrooms or the couch. The music coming from the stereo was soothing and Alvin had the slightest inclination to dance. He realized that the attention had turned to him. The faces were waiting for him to speak. Ellie was prodding him to tell the story.

The story was from his days working with Legal Aid. It involved a young black woman, twenty eight or twenty nine. She was pretty but appeared quite a bit older than her years. It had been a rough three decades. With her was her boyfriend, a roundish gentleman with a mustache and a flavor saver growing just below his lip. They had a story of assault. They wanted to collect damages but hadn't persuaded the DA to prosecute or a civil attorney to take their case.

Alvin explained to them that this wasn't the roll of Legal Aid, but the couple wanted to be heard. Alvin couldn't help but listen. It began one year before. This woman, Natalie was her name, was pregnant with her fifth child. The difference between this child and the previous four being the father. Her husband had sired the previous four. The boyfriend that sat next to her had fathered this last.

The home arrangement was a strange one. The boyfriend lived with them. He payed rent. Even better was the fact that the boyfriend was the husband's brother. The pregnancy had been an uneventful one and she delivered vaginally, but she didn't stop bleeding. They stuffed wad after wad of gauze in her to staunch the flow but nothing worked.

They moved her to the OR, transferring unit of blood after unit of blood along with various blood products to help her clot. Her blood pressure became dangerously low. They opened her abdomen and removed her uterus. Something about it being atonic. The bleeding was stopped.

Natalie was taken to the ICU where she slept quietly with a breathing tube down her throat. Occasionally she would wake up but was not coherent. She was heavily sedated. Her condition stable but still critical. She required medicines to keep her blood pressure up.

Her husband sat outside the OR for seven hours. He sat outside the ICU for thirty six more. He didn't eat and he didn't sleep. He was dressed in a ridiculous looking scrub suit he had donned for the delivery. He saw her twice but she was unable to speak. He just hugged her and cried. He visited the nursery and fed her baby, playing with the tiny fingers, her eyes still barely able to open, a grasping and sucking and helpless little creature.

The third day began and the husband put his wife's daughter to bed. He went three floors down to the ICU. It was visiting hours and he was allowed a brief period to see his wife. There were sixteen beds in the unit, all self contained and glass enclosed, most with a curtain pulled across the front for further privacy.

Natalie was in number nine. He entered and at first thought his wife was under attack by some sort of bizarre euthanizer. Quickly he realized that it was his brother Jerome, the father of the baby, and that he wasn't killing Natalie, he was fucking her. He was humping away on her supine body. Her eyes were open and she did not seem distressed. Her lungs expanded and contracted at the initiation of the ventilator, the endotracheal tube protruding from her mouth like an absurd phallus.

The husband froze, then sprang, ripping Jerome off his wife and beating his face hard into the linoleum floor, streaks of smeared blood contrasting brightly with the antiseptic white of the room. It took two nurses, an orderly, and three guards to pull him from Jerome's nearly unconscious body. Jerome suffered a fractured jaw, two broken ribs, and he lost four teeth.

Jerome and Natalie now wanted to sue her husband for his unwarranted assault on Jerome. Alvin listened intently, filed their paperwork, and quit working for Legal Aid that day.

Everybody laughed uncomfortably as Alvin finished his story. Nancy was the first to speak. "Childbirth seems to be quite the theme tonight. Should we be reading something into that?" She tapped her finger on her bourbon glass as she spoke.

"Only if what you read is that childbirth is painful, life threatening, mucus filled, foul smelling, and generally pretty gross." Alvin smiled at Nancy as he said it. Ellie rapped him lightly on the head.

"Men talk like they have some perspective on and role in childbirth and fertility. Its such a joke. We're the ones on the pill. We're the ones that have our bellies cut open or squeeze a watermelon out between our legs. Men are outside looking in, incidental players who should remain silent." Ellie giggled as she finished, rubbing Alvin's neck gently, becoming drunk and affectionate as the evening wore on. Her eyes were lazy and drooping. The hair that had been so neatly pinned atop her head was now tumbling across her face in random strands. She would blow it out of her face with clumsy upward puffs of breath.

These stories were how they communicated their collective fears, thought Alvin. Fears of poverty and race showing themselves in a guise of humor and entertainment. Stories that were shocking, disgusting, and absurd enough to be real, but distant enough that they reassured the tellers of their select place on the better side of society.

"I must smoke," Alvin said. His intentions stated he moved clumsily towards the patio door. Ellie frowned at him but it was brief. Her drunken face could not maintain an adequate frown for long. It required the coordination of too many muscles. Bill and Ted followed Alvin outside for an excellent tobacco adventure.

The patio was clear of furniture. It was just aging and fading wood, cracking in places, creaking underfoot. The patio looked out on the back yard which was small and surrounded by a chain link fence. The neighboring yards looked the same. Flimsy swing sets were the only things that set them apart. The air was pretty much cold and the sky was black. Unseen clouds hid the moon and stars.

Alvin fired up a butt and Bill and Ted did the same, red embers brightening with each puff. The cherries bobbed up and down with the conversation , leaving small tracers behind, fleeting remembrances of their paths. Alvin smoked hard, enjoying the cigarette immensely, enjoying the cold and the quiet.

Alvin and Bill's friendship was not one where they could joke about Bill's dead wife. Alvin knew this was a lot to ask of a friendship but it was where he wanted it to be. He hadn't known the woman. She'd been dead eight years. Bill had a dry sense of humor. He should be able to make jokes dammit. But Bill never had. Alvin felt it a gulf in their relationship.

"I'm gonna kill her Bill."

"So you've said."

"No, I mean it. Its like I can't breathe. I sure as hell can't think. Its like she's a fly buzzing around my brain, some sort of psychotic nightmare. I can't ignore it."

"People have been known to get divorces before resorting to murder."

Alvin laughed a little. "It just seems like so much trouble."

"Murder or divorce?"

"Divorce. The whole process. Its not like we've dealt with these questions. We'd be starting from ground zero. All the preliminary fights and accusations. We're not what you'd call great communicators."

"Then maybe she's thinking along the same lines. She wants a divorce but is afraid to ask. So she cusses you quietly while plotting your death. A battle royale. Winner take all. We could do it at one of these dinner parties. After the meal of course."

"Yeah, that would be pretty cool. It seems vaguely appropriate. I could get behind that." Alvin envisioned an elaborate mud wrestling scenario, pummeling her bleeding head into the corner post while fans cheered.

Ted had been standing by, silently smoking. Alvin wondered what his take on all this was, how much he understood about the discussion. Ted was quite literal minded. It was hard to imagine what his worst thoughts towards Annette might be. He probably hated himself for days if a sassy put down flitted across his mind. His was a world of unquestioned love and commitment, connected souls destined to be together. Or maybe nobody was like that. Maybe Ted suffered quiet alienation in his own marriage, an alienation that had not yet found its voice.

Alvin smoked his second and looked inside at the women and Brad. They were all seated close together. Women do not like to talk across a room. They like to be near each other, huddled close, passing unspoken messages in some sort of alien code. The key to which was held only by females and perhaps gay men.

Alvin wondered what they were talking about. The men he assumed. Or was that just a male conceit? That what women talk about when men are gone is the debilitating lack of maleness. Maybe they were discussing world events, local politics, clothes, food, furniture.

They were talking about the men. God how this tired Ellie. At the very least they could gossip about the slugs behind their slimy and spineless backs. But no, Jilly and Annette prattled on and on about the perfection that was their mates. Jilly was young enough to believe that Bill had invented sex. Ellie made a mental note to keep this information away from Alvin. Maybe he had forgotten the pleasures of a naive woman. Not likely. As apt to happen as a man forgetting where his penis was. Annette was high on life, as always. Happy at work. Happy in bed. Happy with her twice a day workouts. Ellie needed a stiffer drink.

She watched the men out the window, the easy distance they always kept. Simple smiles were on their faces, not the forced interaction she had come to know too well. Their stances were different when they stood in their packs. Posture, placement of hands, everything was different by the slightest degree. They moved to a different place when they were with other men. A bunch of multiple personality disorders in pretty blazers.

The men came back inside. Alvin felt the warmth of the sudden temperature change and for a moment it was comforting, then not so much. It became slightly suffocating. He took off his jacket and hung it over a chair, rolling up his sleeves. He tended bar for several minutes, freshening things up. He made a martini for himself and brought Ellie a glass of Chardonnay. He sat on the floor with his back against the sliding glass door. He could feel the cool outside air fighting against the warmth on his face. He already wanted another cigarette.

Ellie sat down between his legs, leaning back into his chest. She smelled of lilac and jasmine and, if he concentrated, maybe foot odor. Her body was loose and malleable, just her calves visible beneath her black skirt. She kicked off her shoes revealing her tiny feet bunched up in black hose. She wiggled her toes about. For whatever reason Alvin thought this was sexy. He wanted to tickle the bottoms of her feet and run a finger between her toes. He wanted to scoop her small form up into his arms and cuddle her there, folding her into a small ball, like a cat.

Ted broke the quiet. “We found a really great place in the west part of town. Its twice the size of our place now and the payments are the same. Its one of those little planned neighborhoods out there, a mile outside the city limits. I think we’re gonna buy it.”

Alvin piped up. “Why exactly are you guys moving?”

"Lots of reasons. You know the neighborhood Alvin. Its like its been invaded. Half the houses on our block have been robbed in the last three years. Sometimes we hear gunshots at night. Its just getting scary. We're thinking about kids and it just makes sense to get out, get some security. Besides, it gets us out of this school district."

"But you guys have never been robbed, right?"

"Right."

"And you can pretty much walk around at night without worrying?"

"Pretty much."

"And you can walk to all your favorite restaurants and shops?"

"You know that."

"So what are you running from?"

"What's your point, Alvin?"

"I don't know. I don't mean to be a dick. We've talked about moving farther out too, for most of the same reasons. But then sometimes I think, What the hell am I scared of? By heading out west I give up experiencing any character that this crappy little city has. By making my life ultimately safe I make it ultimately dull. And I think maybe that's why so many people seem so unhappy today. All that white angst. We've so minimized outside stimulation, the interesting and odd and dangerous things in life, that we can only find fault with ourselves or our marriages or our children. But this is complicated by a general inability to see ourselves as the problem so we again look outside for problems. But there is nothing there. We've run from it. So we blame the distant things, the things that rarely affect us. It's the failure of others to maintain a decent and moral world. Social rot. Exotic and mutating infections. When in fact its our failure to remain participants in the real world that has left it so barren."

Everybody was quiet for a moment. Ellie started to giggle. Bill spoke. "Gotten a little drunk have we counselor?"

Alvin was stung for a moment. He wasn't used to expressing those thoughts and he knew he had done it badly. His pride wouldn't allow him to be ashamed in public. He laughed and raised his glass. "To the suburbs and the two car garage."

"Cheers", they said in unison.

"Show them your toy, honey." Ellie poked Alvin in the ribs.

Alvin felt a tingle shoot down his spine. He rose and went upstairs to their bedroom. It was such a different place during parties, abandoned and left behind. Echoes of the real people that lived there padded across the carpet, the people they put away somewhere when company came over. He realized how little this bedroom was his own. It wasn't pink and it wasn't frilly and there was no wicker. Other than that he had left no imprint. The paint, the linens, the bed itself, even the tv had been her choice. The things he gave up to keep the peace.

He found the object of his search in its leather case, tucked a few feet under the bed. He pulled it out and felt its weight, took in the aroma of its oil. He took it downstairs. In the middle of the group he opened the bag and removed his Glock. Lightweight. Cold steel. He showed them the clip and the bullets. He made the cool clicking sound of cocking the gun.

"The great pacifist is armed. I already feel less safe." Bill was laughing at him.

"I just wanted all of you to know that Alvin understands fear too." Ellie was holding the gun as she said it.

"I'm really not sure why I got it. Just because I could I guess. Its like we have this constitutional right to bear lethal weapons and if I don't its almost like not voting, you know. Plus I wanted to have a background check run on me. That sounded pretty cool."

Alvin continued, "I don't know though. I guess I'm afraid of the world. At least a little bit. But I'm more afraid of the gun itself. I mean, it's a much more immediate threat to my life. I think that's why I like it. It makes all the talk of society's decay more real. It brings death in the house."

"You're a barrel tonight honey." Ellie slapped him lightly and picked up the gun. She popped the clip in expertly and cocked the hammer, just to hear the series of noises. Alvin told her to be careful and reached for the gun, pulling it lightly from her drunken grasp. He noted that the safety was off and the barrel was pointed at Ellie's chest.

The world slowed to a crawl. He could see all the faces and their individual expressions, frozen in place, preserved forever in the importance of the moment. He saw the trigger and felt his finger move towards it, as if his hand was operating indepentently of his brain. He saw Ellie's dancing eyes and her falling hair, a few wrinkles were prominent near the corners of her eyes and there was a slight slackness to her chin. He clicked the safety on.

He pulled the clip out and emptied the chamber, putting the gun back in its case. He went to the kitchen and left the gun under the sink. He was breathing a little too rapidly and getting lightheaded. He poured himself a drink and took a long pull. He went outside and lit a cigarette, walking alone into the backyard.

It was colder now because he wasn't wearing his jacket. The clouds had cleared some and he could see a few stars flickering lightly in the corners of his vision. The cigarette didn't last long enough so he lit another, smoking it just as quickly. He felt a little calmer now, if somewhat ashamed and embarrassed. Whether these feelings were due to the evil nature of his thoughts or a response to his cowardice he wasn't sure.

He went back inside and everybody was preparing to leave. He thought for a moment that he had chased them off, then he didn't care. There were frequent handshakes and pecks on the cheek. There were compliments on the food and jokes about the gun. Soon they were all gone and Alvin was alone with Ellie. She smiled at him and they sat down together on the couch. He clicked off the stereo and turned on the tv. The lights were low and Ellie curled up under his arm. Each had an unfinished drink in their hand.

Alvin lit up a smoke and Ellie looked at him in mock horror. She fished in her purse and pulled out one of her own. They both laughed and they both smoked, ashing in a tumbler that was sitting on the coffee table. They finished their cigarettes and Alvin kissed her briefly. She tasted of alcohol and smoke and a touch of heat and for a second he felt very much in love.

"Come to bed with me." Ellie tugged at his arm.

"I'll be up in a minute. I just want to clean up a bit."

"Can't it wait 'till morning?"

"I'll be up in a minute," he said again, seeing in her eyes that she was hurt. He couldn't help himself, though. He couldn't face their bed.

Ellie went upstairs and Alvin watched her walk, her steps slow and deliberate. He picked up the glasses and loaded the dishwasher, turning it on when it was full. He wiped the counters and looked around. Everything appeared surprisingly okay.

He poured himself a final drink and returned to the den, sitting alone in the dark. The only light in the room was the flashing glow of the television set. He watched Sportscenter, comfortable in the routine of it. He sipped and smoked and watched scores and highlights. He needed this. He needed it more than he needed love, more than he needed a wife. He needed this end of the night solitude and deep quiet. He needed to be alone with his tv, his brain more or less turned off.

He spent over half an hour that way, afraid to go upstairs. He smoked six or seven cigarettes, inertia getting the best of him. He finally went up, finding Ellie asleep. Her characteristic snore cut the air. He undressed and hung up his clothes. He crawled quietly into bed next to her. When he laid down he realized how very drunk he was. The room was trying to spin but the sensation soon passed. He closed his eyes and drifted away.

At some point in the night they came together. He didn't know who initiated it. It was more like gravity, a law of nature. It was clawing and pushing, like some kind of fight. But the contestants were so familiar that all suspense was lost. They finished and slept apart.

Alvin awoke with a headache. His mouth was dry and tasted like it was stuffed with cotton balls soaked in elephant shit. His skull felt open to the world, all exposed and pulsing nerves. Fragile. His stomach sent repetitive waves of nausea upward through his body.

He began his breathing exercises, rhythmic, deep, calming. He felt slightly better. His eyes were closed tight, trying to wipe away all thoughts. He rose and went to the bathroom. He splashed water on his face. He looked pale and splotchy in the mirror. His ziplock bag was on the counter, his near empty pack of cigarettes next to it. He lit one and turned on the fan and opened the window. Smoking didn't help.

He showered quickly, coming partially alive. He realized for the first time that it was Saturday, a day of rest. He didn't shave and dressed quickly in sweats and a pullover, sliding his feet into a pair of sandals. He looked at Ellie sprawled on the bed, taking up three fourths of the space. The covers were at her waist, leaving her breasts mostly exposed. Alvin moved to the door, preparing for a morning's breakfast and a slow read of the paper. The thought popped into his head again. He tried to fight it then gave into its power. The flash was brief but unmistakable. Should he kill his wife?

Hawg Calls

Bedtime for Boudica

A (sort of) Tragedy in 4 Parts

Part 1

I have mentioned my nieces before. And the middle one, the 9 year old, the one I call Boo - I mentioned her. "Boo" is short for "Boo-Boo Bear" and she is getting to an age where she isn't so crazy about the name. The problem is that I like it. She is Boo to me. So I decided to switch up her mythology a bit.

I told her that her nickname was no longer Boo-Boo Bear. That she had outgrown it. I was changing her nickname to Boudica. I told her to google it to find out what it meant. I also let her know I would probably call her Boo for short.

The historical Boudica was a Celtic Queen of a tribe called the Icineans in the first century A.D. They call her a "Warrior Queen" because she led an ultimately doomed revolt against the Romans. It's an interesting piece of feminist history. Boo was happy. The Warrior Queen of the fourth grade.

The warrior queen was digging boogers out of her nose and using a rubber band to shoot them at her Uncle Jay from great distances. I imagine the real Boudica never employed this technique on the Romans. Limited supplies of ammunition and all.

Boo's sisters were at separate sleepovers and her parents were skiing. It was just me and the kid. This meant movies she wasn't supposed to watch, loud music, bad dancing and enough candy to make her run around the room seven times and hop up and down on the couch until something got broken. Yeah - I'm THAT uncle. When they're older if they ever get pinched for shoplifting or underaged drinking I'm the guy they are gonna call to bail them out. I find this comforting.

I set up a sleeping bag on the floor in front of the tv so Boo could spend the night there. Boo didn't want to sleep yet since the sugar was still coarsing through her veins like kiddie crack.

She wanted a story.

She wanted to talk about her birthday that was coming up.

She wanted to know why I can't keep a girlfriend.

She wanted me to write down her list of birthday present requests. (A Horse, an Apple laptop computer or a Tivo. I began to think that perhaps I had spoiled this particular warrior queen.)

The Wal-Mart Chronicles . . .

Boo likes my Hog stories. She thinks they make me look stupid. And she likes stories about when grown ups were little kids. So we settled in and I told her my favorite story. About 1978 and 1979. About how all of this insanity started for me. About The Most Painful Game I Ever Remember.

I needed to start at the beginning, to build up to the tragedy that would be the end of my story. I needed Boo to understand how Arkansas had penetrated my soul.

To Boo Arkansas is just a place her grandparents and Uncle live. It has a lake and HORSES! and is excellent to visit. I am not sure she has any idea how far away it is from her home. Distances are a little screwed up in these kids' heads. We talk on the phone whenever we want and sound next door. We video chat by computer and text message and on and on. I think to Boo you just arrive in Arkansas a certain amount of time after getting on a plane. Same with Seattle. Or Colorado. These are destinations without appropriate scales of reference in between. Compare this to the multi-day semi-horrendous vacations we took as children that, while causing unimaginable suffering to untold thousands, certainly helped children learn about the scale and separation of portions of this country.

I wasn't born in Arkansas. I moved to Fort Smith from the Northeast in 1973 when I was 5, about to start kindergarten. I remember it was a long drive and we sang "Bingo" and "On Top of Old Smokey" a lot but not much else.

I suppose things imprint quickly at that age because within a year I remember identifying with the word "Arkansas", like it was part of my name. Just like I could hear my name over and above a throng of voices and realize it meant ME!, that is how I was with the word "Arkansas". For whatever reason I knew it meant ME! and I could always pick it out of a jumble of other words.

My father played sports avidly but was never a big sports "fan". We got into the sports thing slowly, naturally, as a way of feeling our way around a new community. It was an interesting time in Fort Smith.

In 1974 Ron Brewer was leading Northside Highschool to the state title against Marvin Delph and Conway. (right?) In 1975 Brewer moved on to Westark Comunity College in Fort Smith and his coach (Kaundart) came with him. (I assume he had grade issues) I remember seeing him play once, the details are sketchy. I remember the gym being packed. I remember him dunking with his left hand on the break. The game seemed like a major event. People were there to see Ron Brewer. That kind of thing makes an impression.

At some point that year I went to my first Arkansas Basketball game (I think). Seems like it was against A&M and went to overtime. My only other memory is of a guy on the Hogs named Saulsbury or Salisbury or something that reminded me of a tv dinner.

It grew in tiny steps after that but always grew, my identification with the name, the colors, the logo. It wasn't a measurable thing but the relationship was no less real than family bonds.

I remember a babysitter having us listen to Arkansas beat Texas A&M and Scott Bull was the quarterback. Somehow my brain associates that season with the Vietnam War.

We went to the Cotton Bowl in our VW van (SWEET!) and I remember nothing of the game other than thinking Ike Forte was an excellent name. Also my little brother being scared to death by a creepy clown at the Cotton Bowl parade. My brother remains scarred by the experience.

Boo likes that part of the story. The van and her Uncle Lawson crying at the sight of an evil clown. I try to tell her about memories and the way some stick and some don't. That memories are just details. They are paying attention. But they are EVERYTHING because they are all we have. In 1976 my brain wasn't quite ready to soak up everything. But it was opening up. It was about to start forming core parts of my outlook for the rest of my life. Centerpieces to an identity.

The next year we went to Frank Broyles' last game. I seem to recall a gray, dreary affair. And we bought season tickets for basketball and football along with two other families. The timing was phenomenal.

The B-ball team was an emerging phenomenon. They streaked through the SWC undefeated. Marvin Delph was the leading scorer as a junior, Sidney was the emerging star and crowd favorite as a sophomore, and Ron Brewer was my guy. The Fort Smith guy. Details are sketchy to me of that year. I think we only went to 4 or 5 games. I remember Brewer's knee pads and the chants of "Boot, Boot". I remember Sidney's knee socks and it seems like he was always making layups along the baseline. And I remember Marvin's jump shot and the hush of the crowd with anticipation whenever he caught the ball in the corner, ready to let fly.

The hogs played Wake Forest in the first round of the Tourney and Sidney got in foul trouble and we were upset. The first game I ever remember being like a stomach punch.

That same year (actually this part is pretty fuzzy and could have been the year after) I went to my first NCAA Tournament game. Oral Roberts was a first round site (it seems like they had a great gym, really big for a school that size, bigger than Barnhill for sure, could that be true?) and Arkansas folks snapped up tickets in case the Hogs played there - which they didn't. The place wasn't packed but I remember Notre Dame playing. Kelly Tripucka and I think Adrian Dantley and a guy named Duck. It seems like Orlando Woolridge was on that team and maybe Bill Laimbeer but I may be confusing memory with history. Regardless we watched great players and great ball and were hooked for life. The thing that stands out is the crowd repeatedly calling the Hogs. I was thinking that these are MY PEOPLE. OUR PEOPLE. And I recall a sense that the world was not a lonely place. Looking back it was also my first sense of the collective conscious. Of a collective will.

"Why did they call the Hogs if Arkansas wasn't playing?" Boo asked. She likes the Hog Call and is fascinated by the ritual of it.

"It's hard to explain Boo. I guess I don't really know for sure. I do know that it still happens all sorts of places - malls and bars - places like that. It is like a tribal call in a way. Saying "We are HERE! and we are not alone." Maybe it says that we are weak and scared as individuals but together we are fearless. "It's just kind of our thing".

P.S. The more I think about it the more it seems that the tourney game at ORU may have been 1978 and occurred because Arkansas got sent West after losing in the final of the SWC tournament. If so that would make that Notre Dame team the same one we played in the 3rd place game and there is no way Adrian Dantley was on that team. Memory is a very strange and fluid thing.

Part 2

There will always be certain years that define a generation of fans. For many Arkansas football fans it was 1964 and 1965. That was not my time. For many basketball fans it was '89 to '95 just pick your year. I could certainly be in that group (and those were my happiest years) but I had been imprinted long before. For me the years that stick, that made a difference, are 1978 and 1979. I was 9 and I thought things would always be like that.

"Like what?" asked Boo. She was eating licorice and drinking chocolate milk. Probably not going to sleep soon.

"Like we were Kings, Boo. Like we would always be underestimated but always come through. Or almost come through." There was a certain inevitable failure in there too that made it special as well. Be it football or basketball, we were spectacular at times. Everybody was watching. Two SI covers in ONE YEAR. That little razorback logo gave me chills. It was palpable and real.

Lou Holtz took the state by storm in 1977. I think of it as 1978 because that is when they played the Orange Bowl but it was really 1977. Ben Cowins, Ron Calcagni, Dan Hampton, Leottis Harris, Jimmy something whose name now escapes me but whose son is now a running back for Notre Dame (Walker maybe?). Steve Little of course.

That was my first true experience with the Texas thing. I knew the "Hook'em Horns" bit (we lived briefly in Texas when my father was in the Army) but for a little kid seeing the size of the Texas players in their white uniforms highlighted by minimalist burnt orange numbers and logo was a special thing. They looked like gods to me. They were like a negative image of the hogs' colored helmets and jerseys.

The game itself is vague to me. Earl Campbell was huge and strong and brutal. Little had the 67 yard kick and the entire stadium SHOOK as people stomped their feet. A large crowd of like minded people MOVED things. Actually MOVED things.

The Hogs lost and I remember it hurting but I wasn't devastated. It seems like I was equally thrilled by the whole thing. The size and scope of it all. I would soon learn more about the importance of winning. And the inevitability of losing.

I remember the last home game, against SMU I think, and the fans pelting the field with oranges to the point players were kicking them out of the way.

And then the Orange Bowl of course. Surreal. It was a party in our basement. It's hard to believe now that we had only lived in Arkansas for 4 years. It seems as if we had known those families forever. We still know them. Still share tickets. The kids have kids. In some cases the kids have kids in college.

Everything was perfect in that game. Thomas Lott and his bandana were turnovers waiting to happen in the wishbone. Roland Sales took over for the suspended Ben Cowins (a boycott by the black players had been averted I recall) and was unstoppable. Trent Bryant, who later moved to d-back, ran well. Robert Farrell was on that team too, wasn't he? And Houston Nutt came in to mop up as the back up QB, looking uncomfortable with the option. I knew him because he played basketball too. We ended the year ranked #3 in what was and is the foolishness of the college football mythical national championship process.

That was the first full Razorback football season I remember. That is how I thought they went. But even as that was going on my true obsession had already started, Arkansas Basketball.

They had just expanded Barnhill and the tickets we lucked into for hoops were surprisingly close to the court. In fact, within our group we had two front row seats under the basket on the end of the floor towards the visitors bench. This is where Arkansas always shot in the first half and thus warmed up before the game. It was a heaven of sorts and this was my pantheon.

There are few things in the world as impressive as seeing a group of professional or, in this case, near professional athletes up close. Football players are seen from a distance and covered by helmets and pads. Basketball players are much easier to see and appreciate. I was about ten feet away from the '78 basketball hogs and I looked up with awe.

Basketball players are huge to just about anybody, much less a kid, but they move with such easy grace and strength that it really makes them seem to be something other than mortal, or other than the mortals I saw every day. They moved to the goal so softly and were at the rim so easily while I spent so much time and energy just trying to touch the net. I liked just watching them walk. I would imitate the way they casually dribbled the ball when standing around. (I remember Nolan Richardson saying about Matt Jones that he knew he was a great football player and that was how he would make his living but all he had to do was watch him warm up for 5 minutes and he could tell that Matt was actually born to be a basketball player. I thought the same thing the first time I saw Jones dribble a ball and casually put it on the glass. It was his natural sport.)

That '78 team was unbeatable at home. They had grown up together and the crowd had grown with them, learning about basketball the way Eddie Sutton wanted to play it - guard oriented (big guards), all man to man all the time, patterned offense but not as much as people remember. Delph and Brewer were phenomenal outside shooters and had a lot of freedom. Sidney created his own shots off the dribble. Steve Schall was the classic stiff low post guy who actually could score quite well and was always on the verge of foul trouble. Jimmy Counce was the glue guy that never shot unless it was a layup, set screens, and guarded the other team's best scorer. It was a well constructed team except it had absolutely NO depth. (This would be a recurring theme with Sutton teams and drove me nuts. There were some good reasons for it but that is another discussion.)

We had no back up center other than Alan Zahn who was a 6' 7" or so guy that I really don't remember bringing anything to the table other than hustle. James Crockett was the true backup but never got any time in that role.

I loved our backup guards but they were green, green, green. Both were freshmen. One was a kid named Michael Watley who I remember as about 6'2" and solid with a bright future. (His playing time dwindled a bit at the end of the year and he ended up leaving the team. My memory says he transferred to Evansville and didn't have to sit out because their entire team had died in a plane crash. Is that possibly true? Where is the movie about that? What was wrong with the planes in the 70's?) The other backup and by the end of the season the only one was U. S. Reed who had a sweet 'Fro and could leap but had played center in high school (at 6' 3") and wasn't much of a ball handler. (I think Houston Nutt was actually expected to play a big role on that team but between coming in late after the bowl game and what I remember as nagging ankle injuries it never quite worked out. Houston was an interesting ballplayer. Maybe a step slow, looked like a geek but he was actually very flashy and undisciplined. No-look passes and ill-advised shots. He was a fan favorite and make no mistake the guy could play. It's interesting to think about the things that held him back as an athlete now because he may have been one of the best 2 sport players in the state's history.)

"Was his name really U. S.?" asked Boo. "That sounds made up. What did U. S. stand for?"

"It WAS U. S. and as far as I remember it stood for "Ulysses". Like the Union general in the Civil War. At the time it never really made an impression on me what a great name it was. He was just U. S. Reed. He will be important later in this story. Ball handling skills again."

The marquee game of the year was Texas, of course. The interesting thing was that Texas had a fabulous team also. They actually beat us at their place. Their point guard was a kid named Johnny Moore (double zero I think) who became an NBA All-Star until he developed a bizarre fungal form of meningitis. He was fantastic. Their two guard was a scrawny white kid named Krivacs who was a great shooter, like a poor man's Maravich. At forward they had a chubby dude named Ron Baxter who was actually thought of as their best player - good range, good size, good inside. They had LaSalle Thompson as a legit 6'11" center who went on to play well over a decade in the NBA. And then they had some guy who I thought of as the "Bizarro World" Jimmy Counce . He was a clone except he had dark hair. (He is the guy, just out of frame, looking up at Sid dunking on the cover of SI). I think it was an NCAA bylaw at the time that you had to have one of those dudes on your team.

It never crossed my mind that we could lose. The Arkansas basketball team had never lost a game that I had attended and I truly thought the two things were connected. The crowd would not let them lose and I was a vital part of that crowd. The noise would surge at all the right times, carrying defensive possessions, CAUSING steals and dunks it seemed to me.

And Ron Brewer was SO cool. Always. Never flustered. Never mad. Sid was emotional and Marvin was gangly but to me Brewer was the perfect basketball player. The best shot. The best defender. The best demeanor. The coolest look. The best chant when the crowd yelled "Boot, Boot, Boot". (I thought they had invented this sort of thing for him.)

When Sidney made the steal and came flying in for the dunk that would be on the cover of Sports Illustrated (arguably the sweetest basketball photograph ever) he was flying into MY basket and almost landed in MY lap. I still remember the way his momentum slid him around the rim 90 degrees until his head almost hit the backboard. And the way he paused (like he always did) before turning to look back up the court and sprint to get back on defense with that high kneed lope of his.

"Did they win?" asked Boo.

"They always won when I was there." I said. "And Sidney was on the cover of SI and it said 'High on the Hogs - Sidney Moncrief of #2 Arkansas'. And every kid in my class had a poster of it within two weeks."

"Why were you #2?" Boo asked

"Well that was just a poll, Boo. It didn't really matter then. There was a tournament later to see who the best was."

But the thing is that maybe it did matter. We DID win and we WERE awesome and the picture forever burned in my mind and hanging on my wall told me we were #2. And the football team won and dominated and we were #3. I'm not sure what that means. Maybe nothing. Maybe everything in the psyche of the collective.

Part 3

In 1978 it don't think they sold an expensive, glossy program/media guide at the basketball games. They probably did but I never got one. What they did have was something called the Hog Call. It was a newspaper like program the size and form of a thin tabloid and it changed for every game. Each issue would have a full page black and white picture of one of the players. My brother and I collected these for several years and I probably still have quite a few. The photos were always kind of staged and hokey like old fashioned baseball cards but for whatever reason we had it in our heads that a signed picture of Mike Young (awkward reserve shooting specialist) would be valuable some day, sort of like Honus Wagner only not so much.

We stood outside the locker room after one of the games that year, I don't remember which one, Hog Calls in hand. Ron Brewer came outside and talked to us. He was shouting back and forth with Marvin Delph and someone else who was walking around inside the locker room in a towel. Ron was the epitome of 70's cool. He had a leather cap that snapped in the front and a black leather jacket over a sweater and no shirt. The guys in the locker room were calling him "Boothead" not "Boot".

My little brother, always the brave one, asked Ron why they called him "Boot".

Marvin didn't give him time to answer. He just shouted - "Because his HEAD! It's shaped like a BOOT!" And the whole room just rolled with laughter. Brewer just grinned, his teeth big and a little crooked. The coolest of them all. It is an excellent memory.

Boo was getting a little restless, walking on the back of the couch like it was a balance beam, offering me a Sugar Daddy. "Did his head really look like a boot? How could he be so cool if he looked like a shoe?"

I pushed her off the couch and she crashed to the ground with the giggling sound of mild child abuse. "He looked like a COOL boot." I said.

Arkansas went something like 14-2 in the SWC in 1978 and won the conference. (They had been 16-0 in 1977) They were briefly ranked #1 but lost (I don't remember to who, it seems like Baylor but that can't be right) the next day. They were undefeated at home for the second straight year. They were ensconced in the top 10. But something else was going on with that team too. Something that happens at times between a team and its fans.

Special teams and special players TEACH their fans about the game. Bill Simmons (ESPN.com columnist) has talked about this a bit. Larry Bird and the Celtics. Magic and the Lakers. Knicks fans and the early '70's New York teams. These are some examples. It happened with us in '77 and '78. (It happened again from'88-'94)

As fans watching games in person (and to some extent on tv) we began to see the game as the players did, see the FLOOR as the players did. We would see Delph pop open at the same time Brewer did and point to him in the corner. We would see Sidney slide inside his guy BEFORE the shot went up so he would be right there for the put back. The movement and the picks made perfect sense.

With defense we began to see the angles that pressure was creating. How to make a point guard pick up his dribble too high so the passing angle to the wings was too flat. We would see it happen before it happened. As the flustered guard would look for an outlet we would almost break along with Brewer or Moncrief into the passing lane for the steal and the breakaway. The crowd would rise anticipating these things. Willing these things. Just like in the Nolan days when we could sense when a poor kid was dribbling into a trap like a scared and tired mouse. Or Todd Day would pull up for a three instead of going to the hole just because IT WAS TIME. There was a rhythm between crowd and team that was mesmerizing. Or so it seemed to a 9 year old kid. That is why it became impossible to beat those teams at home.

(It is also why so many people were dissatisfied with Stan Heath's teams, even though they may have been improving. They weren't doing those indefinable things that we had learned to expect from Nolan's and Eddie's teams. We saw the passes they should make. We saw the opportunities to press or trap or attack or pull up for the three. We saw plays develop but go nowhere. Maybe we couldn't put it into words but we sensed it nonetheless. It was like dating a perfectly nice girl after divorcing the love of your life. She just couldn't measure up. If Stan had been coaching at a program with no tradition the fans could have learned along with him. But US. We already KNEW.)

The SWC tournament was weird then. It was a 9 team leaugue so they gave the regular season champ (the Hogs) a bye to the finals and the rest of the leaugue played a tournament as usual. This meant that fans didn't travel as much because there would only be one game.

Arkansas played a good Houston team in the finals and my family didn't go. I was pissed. We had to go to the Red Stocking Revue.

The Red Stocking Revue was (maybe still is) an annual charity event in Fort Smith put on by Jr. League types. Kind of a faux burlesque show but mostly with local talent. Some good, some not so much. I recall my mother in a Rockette like kick line and I think she might have been wearing fishnets. I have yet to address the episode in therapy.

Boo spit out a jawbreaker. "Grandma wore WHAT? Are there pictures?"

"Just forget about that part Boo. Wipe it from your memory. Think about Boothead."

"Did she look pretty?" Boo asked, enjoying this part.

"STTOOOPPPP!!! I don't know. I can't think about it. Do you guys have any liquor?"

This was before Walkmans but a few people had radios and scores would percolate through the crowd. Occasionally the emcee would give an update. Eventually he said that Arkansas lost and the air went out of the place. I had to leave and go to the bathroom to keep from crying. (I had gotten to a VERY weird place with that team) It was like hearing that your kid had gone off to college and something bad had happened and you weren't around to do anything about it.

The hogs got sent to the West region because of the loss. I'm not sure what we were seeded. The tourney only had 48 teams then. The bottom 32 seeds played 1st round games and the winners advanced to play the top 16 seeds. We played Weber State in our first game. (As a side note this is the first I recall of sports teaching me American geography and it remained my primary teacher. I learned Weber St. was in Utah and they were in a conference with teams from Montana etc. and that those states were western and near each other. To this day I locate states in my head by conference groupings like the old Big 8 and Big 10. That's why things like the new Big East and ACC drive me nuts). They were not in our class and we cruised. Believe it or not I don't think the game was on tv.

The next game, in the Sweet Sixteen, was the big one. UCLA. You have to know that UCLA was only 3 years removed from John Wooden and his last title. They had certainly fallen but were still big time. The only player I remember is a forward named David Greenwood. A good player who ended up a journeyman pro.

In truth the Bruins had no business on the same court with us. They couldn't handle our pressure and had no anwer for our guards. The problem was they had scouted us and knew our weaknesses. One was depth, the other was the flip side of the "Big Guard" theory. Ball handling.

I may have worshipped Brewer but he was probably a 2 guard playing point and he could be pressured. Sid was shakey on the dribble and Marvin was nearly useless. We were up by 10 or 15 in the 2nd half when they started pressing and we ended up barely hanging on. David Greenwood might have knocked Sid to the floor in that one, briefly knocking him unconscious. Vague memory.

Cal St. Fullerton was next and they must have upset someone but I don't know who. It seems like they had a couple of small, spunky guards. Maybe a dude named Bunch and a guy named Anderson that never missed.

It was a replay of the UCLA game. They couldn't handle us. We were up double digits the whole way until the last 5 minutes when they started pressing. It was MADDENING. In the end their shooter had the ball with a chance to tie (I think) and Brewer knocked it out of his hands as he went up to shoot.

I'm not sure I knew what the Final Four really meant. Just that everybody was really, really jacked about it. And that I was scared of Kentucky.

(I need to make a comment here about the "Triplets" thing. Al McGuire nicknamed Brewer, Moncrief and Delph the "Triplets" before the Final Four. It was the first time it was ever used to my knowledge. That means it was used for all of 2 games during their careers. We (my brother and I) called them "The Three Basketeers" and I have no idea if anyone else did. I admit it was a lame nickname but at least it was generated by the fans watching them in real time. It aggravates me to no end that Arkansas sportswriters have adopted a nickname that was given to the players AFTER THE FACT by the national media and pretend we used it all along. It just never happened. If anyone knows of a nickname used by Arkansas fans or media DURING their career I would love to hear it.)

I was right to fear Kentucky. We couldn't handle them. I remember getting steals and dunks the first 2 possessions and everything going downhill from there. Once Kyle Macy, Kentucky's terrific point guard, got used to the size and pace of Arkansas' pressure it was just a steady, very close beating. They had a post player named Rick Robey who was solid and a swingman name Goose Givens (who I think scored 40 in the title game) who was silky. Macy looked like Beaver Cleaver but was ice. He would always wipe his hands on his socks before free throws to dry them off and half my generation grew up doing the same thing because they had watched him.

It hurt bad but it was a loss. Not a buzzer beater or a bad call. A loss. Life went on.

Two nights later was the consolation game against Notre Dame. This 3rd place game has since been abolished for the obvious reason that nobody cares about it but this one holds a special place in Hog lore. It let my boys go out winners. Brewer won the game backing down to the top of the key and hitting an absolutely perfect turn around jumper from 20 feet. I even remember someone selling a painting of it. The only other thing that stands out from this game is that Jimmy Counce got hurt really bad. Lacerated kidney or ruptured spleen, I don't remember which. I think he was in the O.R. at the end of the game. (Foreshadowing his career as a Cardiovascular surgeon.)

Boo was kicking me in the leg. "Is that it? Is that the most painful loss ever? You don't even seem sad. You didn't even cry. Can I have some ice cream? My stomach hurts. Maybe we should put a towel by my sleeping bag in case I throw up."

"No Boo, that's not the loss. That was just the set up. The background. I needed you to get a feel for where I was at emotionally. Now I'll tell you about the BIG loss."

"Finally"

"And I'll get you a bucket instead of a towel."

Part 4 (Big Finish)

Boo was running with scissors. She's that kind of kid. She runs with scissors just because she knows I won't stop her. She was giving me a haircut since she had accidentally gotten gum stuck in my hair.

"Finish your story while I make you look nice" she said with a very serious expression. "I need some tissues though. In case you start bleeding again."

The life of a hog fan kept rolling right along in 1978. I turned 10 and when football season hit the team was on the cover of the SI college football preview issue. "Calcagni, Cowins and Holtz" it said, #1 at Arkansas.

Now the way I remember it is we moved the Texas game to the first game of the year for tv, but I lost a bet on that subject earlier this year when we looked up the results in the Arkansas media guide. I would still swear it was the first game of the season but there it is right in that guide. Memory fails again.

Regardless, we blew our ranking with a loss to Texas in Austin. This could be blamed on the SI cover jinx or on the fact that we wore red pants on the road. Either would be fine. We followed up that loss with a loss to Houston at the Astrodome. A game I attended which was kind of cool but a serious butt kicking. Again this was entirely due to the fact that we were wearing RED PANTS. Now I realize they look really good but COME ON PEOPLE. Think about the children.

Otherwise it was a really good season with blowout win after blowout win and a top 20 ranking. We ended up playing UCLA in the Fiesta Bowl. (At that time there were 4 New Year's Day Bowls - Rose, Cotton, Sugar, Orange. The Fiesta was the most prestigous after that probably). We tied. Summed up the year pretty well.

We were right there. On the cusp. But couldn't get over. It was fun watching though. I was waiting for basketball season anyway.

The 1979 basketball season was one that would have huge problems but I was too young and stupid to realize it. We lost the core of the team from the previous year. We had Schall back at center which, while not a negative, certainly scared noone. The thing was we had Sidney. That was all that mattered. The state worshipped Sidney like it has no athlete I can remember except maybe Matt Jones. And Sid was a bigger winner than Jones ever dreamed of being. He was cool, classy, hard nosed and home grown. He was better loved even than Corliss it seems to me.

But Sidney had to CARRY that team. And he had to do it with severe tendinitis in both knees. For a guy who's entire game revolved around his explosiveness this was a big liability. The first half of the season he eked by on smarts and experience.

The rest of the lineup was U. S. Reed, who played a form of point guard but wasn't a natural at it in any way, Alan Zahn, who was an athletic 6'7" and a good defender and rebounder but didn't give us much on the offensive end, and Scott Hastings, a surprisingly good 6' 10" freshman with a little bit of range. The only reserves of note were Tony Brown, a 6'6" freshman guard who backed up both positions and Mike Young a slow shooter off the bench. Keith Peterson was a heralded freshman from Parkview but he got crossways with Eddie and didn't get any playing time until his sophomore year. Crockett was still there and still struggled.

(I should say here that Hastings ended up being a long time mediocre pro and is still a much loved color guy for Nuggets games. Tony Brown managed an improbable journeyman career. Working his way from the CBA into the NBA where he stuck for several years. Steve Schall was drafted but never played in the NBA. And of course, until Joe Johnson puts together another 4-5 years of his current level of play, Sidney is the best NBA player ever to come out of the University of Arkansas. So this team was not without talent.)

So what we had was a very young team with Big Guards, poor ball handling, terrible outside shooting, excellent low post scoring and the chance to be a good defensive team. Reed was the only starter that could hit a deep jumper. (Sidney had a mid range shot but that was all.) This was a perfect example of the kind of team Eddie Sutton molded into a competitive squad.

They lost games. I remember being stunned by that. Some of them they lost badly. When Texas came to Barnhill things were going to be ramped up to a whole new level. Something like a 24 game home winning streak was on the line. They had basically the whole team back from the year before except for maybe Krivacs. They were very good and very seasoned. And then the roof caved in. I got invited to a birthday party.

"What's so bad about that?" asked Boo. "I like birthday parties. At least you had friends then. Put your chin down Unk. I just dropped my gum again."

"Ouch! Stop pulling my hair. And I have friends now. Sort of. They just don't have birthday parties. At least my friends have jobs. Well, most of them do. That's more than I can say for your crew of fourth grade losers. Ouch! Is there blood on my shirt?"

Danny Barge had the birthday. The same night as the Texas game. Danny was a friend and a good guy but it wasn't like we were BEST friends or anything and I took pains to explain this to my mother at length. She didn't care. I was going to the party. I still carry a grudge.

Of course Arkansas lost. I WASN'T THERE. You have to understand that somewhere in my brain I actually think I had developed the belief that there was a real cause and effect. That the crowd, the HOME CROWD, wasn't complete without me and thus lacked its full power. It was a childish concept and one I am sad to have lost.

They lost another home game that year, I'm not sure to who. Sid got in a semi-brawl against A&M. Things very nearly unraveled. But they didn't.

The SWC tourney changed its format that year so that Arkansas had a bye into the semis. The tournament was in Houston and my family went. The Hogs had evolved a defensive style of play with a deliberate offense that revolved around Sidney and Schall with a little help from Reed and sometimes Hastings. Rare subs and very slow pace.

When we showed up for the tourney our tickets actually ended up in some added seats in folding chairs DOWN ON THE FLOOR under the goal. First and second row. We always got lucky like that back then. I remember people calling the hogs all over town, everywhere we went. We seemed to own the arena and the city of Houston.

We beat Texas in the final in a game that I swear was 39-38 or something like that. (Remember no three point line and no shot clock) The whole thing was a blast.

There used to be a monthly glossy magazine called "Arkansas" magazine (I think that is what it was called- maybe it was quarterly). When it came out a month later and had a photo spread about the game there was a picture of my brother and me. We were both standing and yelling, doing upside down horns, wearing some kind of trucker baseball caps with hog logos, hog t-shirts tucked into jeans and, for some reason, green sweat bands.

"Why were you wearing sweat bands?" Boo asked. She was trying to braid a couple of wispy strands of my hair.

"Because we were cool."

"I doubt it" said Boo as she used a rubber band to give me the first of a series of tiny dreadlocks sctterED across my scalp. "What is cool about sweat bands?"

"Its hard to explain. I think we kind of wanted to let everyone know that we weren't your average fan. That we were ballplayers too, you know. We were ready for action. It was the '70's Boo. These were very confused times for everybody."

We went to the NCAAs on a roll, playing very well. Again we had to wait for a first round game to see who we would play. Amazingly we ended up with Weber State again. I was starting to think that there was more than one Weber State and that this was just a generic name they gave to semi-crappy teams of five white guys that you had to beat in the first round of the NCAA tournament before you got to the REAL games.

We played them in Lawrence, Kansas and we went to the game with some friends (we had a full-on hoop jones at this point). The only thing of note that happened (besides Mr. Robinson's speeding ticket and his lengthy explanation of the evils of "speed traps") was that Larry Bird and #1 ranked and undefeated Indiana State played in the same Arena in the game before the hogs.

I had heard of Bird, of course, and I hated him on principle. I'm not sure what those principles were. I'm just sure that they were very strong and very convincing.

"You hated Larry Bird?" screeched Boo the Boston girl. "I thought we loved Larry Bird."

"This is a subject I haven't brought up before to avoid conflict between the families, Boo. But the fact is that Larry Bird, while being a very good ball player, is evil and probably should have been destroyed shortly after birth."

"He's ugly" said Boo.

"Yes he is" I answered. "You get right to the heart of the matter, Boo. That's one of the things I've always liked about you."

I remember wanting to not be impressed by Bird. And I wasn't until I realized he put up and effortless 30 points and 10 or so boards. That was how he played. He dominated quietly. At least to a kid's eye. He was carrying a team of NOBODIES to an undefeated season and #1 ranking. It was like Arkansas State being #1. That's how good he was. But he had a very cheesy mustache and a bad complexion. These things were important.

The sweet sixteen was in Cincinnati and we played a powerful Louisville team. They would win the national title the next year. Darrell Griffith (Doctor Dunkenstein) was their star. They had Scooter McCray too. It was practically a home game for them. This was the first of a long series of Arkansas/Louisville NCAA matchups (a rivalry that is never talked about). We crushed them like grapes.

It was all coming together. Sid was in another world. He couldn't be stopped. My father had entered some sort of basketball dementia. We all piled in our red and white Suburban and drove to Cincinnati the next day.

There remained the matter of the tickets (as in we didn't have any and the game was sold out). We pretty much just sent my mother out on the streets of Cincinnati with a wad of cash and instructions to get some. We don't ask what she did to get them. Some things aren't important. You prioritize in this world.

She was happy to do it. She loved Sidney more than the rest of us. She liked Scott Hastings too, which I thought was creepy. If she could have adopted U. S. Reed I would have had an older brother. My mother loved her some U. S. Reed.

"Would he be Uncle U. S. ?" asked Boo. She was experimenting with eye shadow on me. She thought my eyes looked "tired".

We played the evil Larry Bird and Indiana State for a return trip to the final four. The place was rocking. Our seats sucked. Bird , despite looking like someone that should register as a sex offender, was unstoppable.

"What's a sex offender?" asked Boo.

"I think you need to put lip gloss on me, Boo. I want to sparkle."

The game was tight the whole way. Bird was lighting us up. Finally with about 10 minutes left Sutton decided to put Sid on Bird. He more or less shut him down the rest of the way. That is how good Sidney was. Bird still ended up with 30 but Sid almost played him point for point (he had 25 or so) AND he guarded him in crunch time.

It came down to a tie game with about a minute and a half left. Remember, no shot clock (which was a serious flaw), so we were holding for the last shot. I was so nervous I was going to puke. We were NOT a good ball handling team. But if we got the ball to Sid late it was ballgame baby.

Reed was the point and he was awkward at that stage of his career. All legs. Like a colt. He was being guarded by Carl Nicks who was a thug point guard of no discernible talent made good by being a teammate of Bird's. The kind of player you love if he is on your team and hate if you are playing against him. He was a bulldog. Played with his hands and body a lot. After the game my father kept referring to him as "That f*****g criminal". That kind of player. (This might be a good time to note that my father had lost all perspective on things as well)

"Grandpa said what?" yelped Boo. Trying to see if my overall look was symmetric. She seemed satisfied.

"Do you have any hair dye? I think we should make me a blonde." I said. Boo clapped her hands and ran upstairs.

Reed was in the far corner, near half-court. I don't think he had used his dribble yet. Nicks was in his face. Reed was jab-stepping to get him off. Reed went to the floor still holding the ball. Then he stood up. The whistle blew.

There could be only two calls. Either he was tripped and fouled or he traveled because you cannot stand up without traveling. Obviously we thought he was tripped. Would SWEAR he was tripped. (I actually have no idea) Would SWEAR AN OATH IN COURT HE WAS MUGGED AND TRIPPED.

What I do know is that Reed, with those long legs, looked like a newborn foal struggling to stand, weak and confused, everything slipping away. Sidney would not even get a chance to touch the ball.

The game wasn't over but it seemed that it was. Indiana State held the ball and tried to get it to Bird but Sid was all over him. The ball ended up going to this sad sack CHUMP named Bob Heaton in the lane. I looked away at this point. I couldn't watch. I just couldn't. It was that painful. I had NEVER seen them lose.

But I have seen film.

Heaton threw up an off balance left-handed (I don't know if he was left handed or not, I think not) dog shot that crept in as the clock went to zero. Steve Schall is standing under the basket making the "timeout" sign over the ball with the universal "I can't believe we just lost" look on his face.

History was changed that day. Indiana St. beat a weak Depaul team with a freshman Mark Aguirre in the final four. We would have crushed Depaul. We probably could not have handled Michigan State and Magic in the final but it must be said that they played what was then an unusual defense (now played by everybody), a matchup zone that befuddled Bird. Texas played the same defense and we had played them 3 times that year and were used to it. The point is that the legendary Bird/Magic rivalry would not have gotten off the ground. Who is to say what happens then?

I should have watched the last shot. It might have made the difference. I lost faith with the team. Fear got the best of me. It was my fault. I failed them. I was a coward.

All because of that f*****g criminal.

""What did you call him Uncle Jay?" Boo asked.

"Nothing Boo. How do I look?"

"You look very, very pretty. And I liked your little story. That Sidney person sounds nice."

"He was nice Boo. I miss him. And yes I do look pretty."

A Shoe Story

"If dreams are like movies, then memories are films about those."

The Counting Crows (Mrs. Potter's Lullaby)

Somewhere in my mind I hear the squeak of my basketball shoes on the gym floor. That is the strongest memory I have of my pathetic little athletic career. I love that sound. I'm not so sure I loved it back then but I desperately love it now.

During practice we would spit on the floor then rub the treads of our shoes in the saliva to get the perfect bite from our hightops. We did this all practice long, hundreds of times a day. It was like some sort of giant microbial cesspool, a TB experiment gone horribly wrong.

When we got too dry we would dribble water from our mouths at the water fountain to make a good puddle on the ground and then squeak our way through that. TRULY EXCELLENT TRACTION!

For games we somehow found our manners and would lick our fingers and wipe the bottoms of our shoes. I don't see professional players do this. Do they maybe have somebody who licks their shoes for them? I would probably do it if I could be in Sam Cassell's posse. Maybe their shoes are just a little bit better than mine. That would figure.

Nothing was better than the feel of a clean basketball floor and a leather ball perfectly inflated. The gym empty and only partially lit with the bleachers pushed back into the walls. The extra goals would be hanging down, screaming "WE PLAY BASKETBALL HERE!". Every dribble would bounce perfectly and echo forever.

I own Danny Fortson's shoe. There I said it. His right shoe. Game worn. I know this because it came with a piece of paper that tells me so. I don't think he got to play much in that game because the shoe looks pretty fresh. It is a big shoe and it is signed but it is not superhuman big, maybe a 15 or 16. It is the centerpiece of my living room. This shoe sits in a glass case between my two tvs. You DO know who Danny Fortson is don't you? I hope so. Nobody else seems to. They all just think I'm weird for having it.

Memories are strange. I remember the squeaks on the floor and the ballgames and everything was happy. I rarely think about how much I dreaded practice every day, how these men that were supposed to be teaching me about sport and life instead just taught me that if I wanted to play the game I loved, first I had to survive. I HATED almost all of my coaches. They took the fun out of basketball, which I thought was impossible. At the time I thought the things they did to us bordered on abuse, approached the line of cruelty. I'm not entirely sure anymore. But maybe I am

When my brother was in ninth grade one of the coaches lined up four of the kids (including my brother) and began swatting them with a big paddle as part of a "Kangaroo Court". It was supposed to be funny

The next day my brother and one other kid could barely walk because the backs of their legs were swollen with hematomas and the skin was split. Everybody still thought it was kind of funny. My Mom didn't.

In front of the whole class she laid hands on that coach and asked if he wanted HER to swat HIM. He just stood there, always a weakling and a coward when not intimidating children.

Fortson's shoe was a gift from my brother. Sports are important between us. Basketball says things that words cannot. Nobody understands why he bought me Danny Fortson's shoe, even after I explain it to them. I explain it to women as a sort of test, to see if they "get it". They don't. Kind of like when I was in my twenties and I would have women read "Fisher's Hornpipe" and see if they laughed at the right places. They never did.

See, the thing is that it doesn't HAVE to be Danny Fortson's shoe. It could be almost anybody's shoe. As long as they aren't a superstar or my favorite player or something like that. It needs to be the shoe of somebody who is kind of anonymous now, almost a nobody. But at some point, at some level, they were a STAR. They meant something in the sports conversation if you were paying attention. They remind us of a specific time and place because they never went anywhere else. Danny Fortson was a BEAST at Cinncincinnatti. He's an undersized, overpaid hothead now. These things are important in my world. If someone understands who Danny Fortson is then I know they are in my tribe. Do you see?

The shoe could be Ledell Eackles' (which would be way cool!), or Jerald Honeycutt's. It could be Chris Washburn's or maybe Derrick Chievous' or the crown jewel, Fennis Denbo's. It just has to take you to a place that few can go. Do you see?

In Arkansas lore it would be Lawson Pilgrim's or David Scott's or Trey Trumbo's. Maybe James Crockett's or Ray Biggers'. Do you see?

I love the echo of a dribbled basketball. It is the sound of footsteps in Valhalla. When I close my eyes to sleep I see a crowded gym. Two dozen balls are bouncing at random. I try to synchronize their beat until it is a syncopated rhythm. Do you remember that? When it would happen ever so briefly. All the balls being dribbled in unison. Maybe one just slightly off so the sound was like that of heart valves closing, perfect but not simultaneous.

And then the rhythm breaks down and it all becomes random again and I wonder if I imagined it to begin with. In some ways that is basketball to me. Or maybe that is life to me. I get confused sometimes.

Danny Fortson's shoe is a bridge to things, a bridge to basketball, to my brother, to humility, to the tribe of sport. Sports are a bridge as well. Not a wall, not a moat, they are no kind of barrier.

Does this mean I'm looking for a Cinderella to fit into Danny Fortson's shoe?

Betting Man

The Wal-Mart Chronicles . . .

"The screen door slams. Mary's dress waves.

Like a vision she dances across the porch as the radio plays."

-Bruce Springsteen- "Thunder Road"

My bookie came by today. She brought lemon squares. I thought that was nice. She's a nice person, my bookie. Her job can get a little depressing sometimes, especially on collection day (Tuesdays), so she tries to brighten things up with baked goods. I, for one, appreciate the effort.

It's raining outside as she stands in my doorway, water dripping from the sides of her umbrella. She is wearing a sweatshirt and jeans and her hair is in a tousled short 'do that is stuck somewhere between Dorothy Hamill and lesbian softball player. One foot in one world, one foot in the other. It kind of suits her in many ways.

I was a little surprised to see her since she actually owed me money this week. Usually in these situations she will just call and see if I want to roll the balance over to next week. I usually do. I think this must be an old bookie trick because it seems like I pay in quite often but she never pays out.

She wants to talk about her son. This is something that we do on occasion. We share his miserable little triumphs in this frighteningly large world. We talk about the tiny failures that cut her to the quick. This is the type of bookie I have. And she is having, it would seem, a pretty good day.

Our relationship is not strictly bookie/bettor. I referred her to a doctor in Oklahoma City once to get worked up for Lupus. Occasionally over the years she has asked me to treat her boy for strep throat and the like. You do this sort of thing for your bookie, just like you do it for cops. Because they seem sad and lonely. Because you just never know. It is best to stay on their good side.

We settle down in my living room with her lemon squares and glasses of milk. Her milk is spiked with scotch because that's the way she likes it and because she is a hopeless alcoholic. My milk is not because that just seems sort of gross.

I tell her about the perfect moment I had over the weekend. I mention the Arkansas game. She laughs and sips her drink. (She makes a killing on Hog games because people bet with emotion and skew the line. This week all the locals were betting against the home team.) I tell her about the moment McFadden popped to the outside and had nothing but daylight in front of him for 80 yards. I explain that it isn't the WHOLE run that is perfect but just that MOMENT, right before he is in the clear when you know he is about to explode by someone, when he actually seems to be running DOWNHILL. It is graceful and powerful and entertaining and it is something to behold. It is sport as perfect as it can be.

"You guys" she said, shaking her head dismissively.

"What?" I asked.

"When you dudes touch yourselves do you think of DMac?" she laughed.

She is talking now about her boy, Ronnie, who is about 16. Apparently the kid is on the basketball team at the small high school he attends. This in itself is amazing to me because Ronnie is an ODD child. Very odd. Precociously odd as a matter of fact.

There was a time when they thought he was autistic (and I think he probably is just a bit) but he didn't fit in any diagnostic categories. The doctor that did his neuropsyche tests said that the kid was just "weird". I must concur with that diagnosis.

He wears nail polish and I don't know if I have ever seen him without a watchcap on. He makes strange noises when he is concentrating. He is scrawny and hyperactive and bounces around like a spring loaded tendon. He smells faintly of moldy bread and Pledge. He has been arrested twice for exposing himself to cattle. Also, he likes to shoot a basketball.

She asked me once to talk to Ronnie about some of his "issues". Ronnie's first words to me when I went up to his room were "Why'd they pick you? Are you the local expert on beastiality?" I doubt it's easy being the son of an alcoholic female bookie. I think your psyche develops some inner friction.

Apparently his school had an intrasquad game as part of their preseason. Because of numbers Ronnie was virtually guaranteed to play. It would probably be the only time all year he would see any action.

"So there is this one moment in the 3rd quarter." My bookie is telling me the story. She is excited and animated and there is powdered sugar on her mouth from the lemon squares. "Ronnie catches the ball on the wing and before he ever makes a move I know he is going to shoot it. He is just like that. But when he gets the ball - it was like for that 5 seconds he became another person. The angles of his face softened and he seemed calm. He took one dribble to the right and let an absolutely perfect jumper go. It was good all the way, Jay. Beautiful. And Ronnie didn't jump around like some freak after he made it. As soon as it left his hands he started to sidestep back up the court because he knew it was going down. Then he just turned and jogged like he had made that shot a dozen times before. As he's jogging down the court he glances over at me - I'm screaming at this point - and pushes his palms toward the ground. Telling me to relax, calm down. But he did it with a smile. I swear to you Jay, for just those few moments I think my life was perfect."

We sat there for a few minutes more, eating lemon squares and drinking milk. Van Morrison was playing on my stereo and the song was "Wonderful Remark". We thought of those moments -the arc of a jump shot, the smile of a child, the voice of Van Morrison, the lyrics of Bruce Springsteen.

Then she got up and left quietly, stumbling half drunk out into the pouring rain. Her umbrella was pushed out in front of her, holding off the wind and the cold wet sting of the afternoon storm. She had people to see.

Bottle Cap Thieves

The Wal-Mart Chronicles . . .

"In ancient times cats were worshiped as gods;
they have not forgotten this."
-Terry Pratchett-

Years ago I had two cats. I don't have them anymore. They went away. Cats are like that sometimes. They don't do something so dramatic as die. Things such as that are beneath them. They just go away and leave their legacy open ended.

I got them as kittens when I started med school in '91. We lived together in a tiny apartment in Little Rock. They never went outside because there was too much traffic in the neighborhood. As far as they knew the whole world was air conditioned.

They were brothers (litter mates) and best friends. They were my companions during med school, hanging around my Big Chair as I studied, purring in my lap as I napped, shredding my curtains for no apparent reason, pooping and urinating in various corners in clear violation of the "Litter Box Doctrine", standing at the door whenever I got home, pretending to greet me but actually making a break for the outdoors and FREEDOM!, scrambling in fear from my squirt gun, knocking things off my tables because it was always important to take off from a sitting position really, really fast, shedding hair 24 hours a day 7 days a week coughing up strange things from the depths of their intestines, scaring me as they jumped on top of my shower to watch with amazement as I covered myself with the water they themselves so feared, making me feel kinda weird because they were seeing me naked, possibly engaging between themselves in the love that dare not speak its name, staring at me with that singular look of big-eyed cat disdain every time I tried to explain that they needed to "Get Down", and stealing my bottle caps.

That's right, stealing my bottle caps.

I used to drink quite a bit. I don't drink at all anymore but that is another story. Back in those days I liked to sit in my really big chair and sip beer and smoke cigarettes and study and watch basketball. It was all very sophisticated. And since it was sophisticated I drank imported beer and I drank it from bottles. That's just how I rolled. (I think if I met my 1993 self today I probably wouldn't like him very much but that is also another story. I think he would also wear much smaller pants than I do.)

When I twisted or popped the caps off of these bottles of beer I would just drop them next to my Big Chair, with the idea that I would pick them up later. But I never had to pick them up. They just disappeared. I didn't question this. I didn't think it was magic or anything like that. I just thought they were falling into whatever vortex or wormhole ate my socks and remote controls. This made sense to me at the time.

So my cats and I watched the '92-'93 Razorback Basketball season together. This was the season prior to the National Title team and it remains my favorite Arkansas sports team of all time. It was Che and Goo's favorite basketball team as well, though they both preferred tennis due to the rhythmic ball movement. Che and Goo were the cats' names. Actually their full names were Che Guevara and Augusto Sandino. Che and Goo for short.

You might ask why I named my cats after dead Latin American communist revolutionaries. You could just as easily ask why I had a ponytail, an earring and wore flannel all the time. Some questions have no adequate answers.

The team that season was everything that a Nolan Richardson team could be. They were smothering on defense and streaky on offense, unbeatable one night and horrible the next. They had a budding superstar in Corliss but the rest of the team was a weird amalgamation of juco talent and lightly recruited "finds". People always talked about Nolan having the best "athletes". I always thought this was a way of belittling the accomplishments of his teams because they were rarely "athletic" in the true sense of the word. Scotty was too slow, as was Corey Beck. Clint McDaniel could barely dunk. I'm not sure I EVER saw Dwight Stewart get over the rim. Roger Crawford was a pretty good athlete but barely average for the SEC. Darrell Hawkins was a great leaper out of high school but injuries slowed him down before he ever got any real playing time. Robert Shepard was extraordinarily quick with his hands. Warren Linn and Davor Rimac were two of the best athletes on the team in terms of quickness and jumping but nobody ever wanted to notice because they were white. The simple fact of the matter was that the players on those teams excelled because they played harder with a better plan than anybody else.

That team beat Penny Hardaway's Memphis team at home. They beat Missouri and Arizona on the road. After a mid-season swoon they upset Kentucky in Bud Walton and Darrell Hawkins jumped on the press table and pumped his fist at the crowd.

At its best that team was like crazed dogs. They would have 10 to 15 steals a game. Robert Shephard, Clint McDaniel and Corey Beck TERRORIZED opposing guards to the point that they would throw the ball up for grabs because they didn't want it any more. Shephard in particular went wild that year. He had a couple of games that he simply took over defensively. It was beautiful to watch. His arms were so long it looked like he could tie his shoes without bending over. And his hands were so quick and strong the guys he was guarding would look violated after games.

Che and Goo would listen to me scream and yell all season long. Sometimes they would scramble away in fear because of my outbursts but more often they would just look at me with feline disgust and the go back to licking each other. That was our system.

When the Hogs went to the NCAA tournament they blew out Holy Cross in the first round. In the second round they played St. Johns and actually played bad most of the game but made a little run to take about a 6 or 8 point lead with about a minute and a half left and St. Johns just quit because they were tired of getting beat on. They didn't foul or anything. They just quit. It was one of the most extraordinary things I have seen in college basketball.

And so this completely revamped team of odds and ends and a somewhat injured freshman all-american (Corliss) made it to the Sweet Sixteen to play the #1 team in the country, North Carolina. That was the team that beat Michigan and the Fab Five in the final game when Webber called the famous timeout they didn't have. UNC had Eric Montross, Derrick Phelps, Brian Reese, George Lynch, Donald Williams and a few more. They were stacked but had actually been an underachieving group so far in their college careers.

The night of that game was one of those nights that just seems to stand out in my life. It had sharp edges. Beginnings and endings.

We finished a series of tests that day so I had absolutely no studying to do over the weekend. I tried to convince the woman I was in love with to stay in town for the weekend and watch the game with me but she decided to go home and try to convince the man she was in love with to leave his wife. I decided I wasn't drinking nearly enough.

I went to a sports bar with a friend who graduated from Vanderbilt. Vandy had a fantastic team that year with Billy McCaffery and had won the SEC. They were in the Sweet 16 as well. By the time the Hogs tipped off I was urging my buddy to sing a Phil Collins song on Karaoke, I was hitting on an extremely questionable looking and dentally challenged waitress, and Vandy had been upset. I held out little hope for my beloved Pigs.

I was wrong. They came out on fire. Shephard buried deep shots. Phelps couldn't handle the pressure. UNC couldn't get into their sets and thus couldn't pound us inside. We were up double digits before I knew what was happening. The whole bar was standing and screaming with every possession. We were also just waiting for UNC to wear the Hogs down.

Eventually they did. Early in the second half Carolina evened things up and I was sure the Hogs were doomed. But they bounced right back into the lead and went punch for punch with the best team in the country. Right down to the last possession when Carolina pulled out to a three point lead and Arkansas got the ball back with a chance to tie. Shephard panicked for what seemed like the first time all year and got caught in the air and traveled. Ball Game.

It was a weird feeling after that game (besides the nausea and drunkenness). I had rarely if ever been that sure before a game that the Hogs would lose so I wasn't crushed. And I'm not sure if I have ever been as proud to be a fan of a team as I was to be a fan of that group of players. At the same time they were done. They had lost. And I was alone.

A friend dropped me off at my apartment and I went in through the back door. I went in this way quite a bit as it was closest to the street. It was actually a patio and then a sliding glass door into the apartment. On this night the door was WIDE open. It was so unusual that at first it didn't quite register. But soon enough it did. I'd been robbed.

My TV was gone, my computer was gone, my stereo was gone, all my CDs were gone. Even worse Che and Goo were gone. I spent an hour looking for them and after the cops left I spent the rest of the night walking around the neighborhood calling their names and whistling (as if they had ever come when I called). I never found them. It was that kind of sharp edged day. One where your favorite team loses, your girl chooses someone else, and your pets run away. It makes an impression.

The next day I was digging through the closet where I kept their litter box, looking for an old stereo I had stashed away. I needed something to pierce the silence. In the far corner, under a cardboard box, were hundreds and hundreds of bottlecaps, horded like nuts in a tree.

Until I graduated and moved out I would randomly find bottle caps in that apartment. They would show up under the bed or in the kitchen or near the couch. Maybe it was magic or a vortex but every time I found one I thought of those cats and those Hogs.

In Search of a Nemesis

The Wal-Mart Chronicles . . .

"I had nothing to offer anybody except my own confusion."

Jack Kerouac

I don't have a nemesis right now. I think to have a fully satisfying life one needs a good nemesis. Now, I'm not talking about an enemy. I probably have a few of those. A nemesis is something altogether different and more important, more akin to a rival, something like a love/hate relationship. A person who's life parallels your own but surpasses it in subtle yet infuriating ways. It's even better if this person is very nice and in no way deserves the bitterness and enmity you feel towards them, the guilty pleasure you take in their failures. This is such a common and necessary part of life that Germans have a word for it, "schadenfreude" which translates as "taking pleasure in the misfortune of others." That's how it translates but it is an inadequate description.

The reverse is also true with a nemesis, and probably more important. I think it was Oscar Wilde who said "Every time a friend succeeds I die a little." Or maybe it was Woody Allen. Regardless, inner conflict and guilt make life worth living.

I had a nemesis in high school, a couple actually. One was for sports and girls. another for school. This made things kind of awkward because while each individual nemesis would surpass me in their specific category I could always rationalize that I could dominate them in the area outside their specialty. It weakened their hold over me.

College was different. I lacked a nemesis because I was going through a distinctly non-competitive phase of my life. This was due in large part to chemicals, reggae, and the fact that I was in California. It's hard to have the energy for a nemesis when it's 78 degrees every day and you're burning incense and listening to Bob Marley.

But aahhhh med school! That was nemesis heaven. You couldn't swing a dead cat without hitting a nemesis there. It was like they were breeding them. We studied together while secretly hoping for the other guy to tank so we could bump up a notch in class rank. Constantly tried to upgrade girlfriends. Pretended like we didn't have to work to maintain our grades. Good Times!

Things have been lean since then, what with adulthood and all. But a new guy moved in down the block about six months ago and I've had my eye on him. I think he's perfect. Friendly, accomplished. His house and yard are better than mine. He has pets and children. He's a doctor too but he's a CARDIOLOGIST. He has charity events at his house. His wife is WAY better looking than anything that wanders through my place. The cops never go to HIS place because the neighbors hear weird sounds. He is always jogging or biking around. In fact, he may be TOO GOOD to be my nemesis. I may just have to run up to him, push him to the ground and run away.

We need a good nemesis for Arkansas basketball. Kentucky will do for a team but I'm talking about a player, someone that we know and love/hate, someone like Penny Hardaway.

I have to say a few things first. The 1993 basketball team is my favorite all-time team. Even more so than the '78 team or the national title team. After '92 I was convinced our run was over. I thought Day, Mayberry and Miller were a once in a dozen years miracle and we wouldn't see that sort of talent again. Before '93 I loved Nolan. After '93 I worshipped him.

It actually happened in late '92, the first game of the year, I think, but I'm not sure. We opened with Memphis State, the same Memphis State team that had bounced our great MayDay team in the second round of the NCAAs about 8 months before.

Memphis State was our nemesis as a team and Penny Hardaway was our nemesis as a player and man was he beautiful to watch. If you don't remember that time we were in a horrible spot. Memphis had a top ten team, virtually everybody back from an Elite Eight squad. Penny was a junior (I think) and they had a 6'10" kid named David Vaughn who was a sophomore who had KILLED us in the tourney as a freshman and looked like he was going to be a big time pro.

On the flip side we had lost just about everything. We had Darrel Hawkins back, but he had never been anything but a role player. Robert Shephard was back but he had been a disappointment the year before. One of the missing elements that nobody talks about regarding the last season of the MayDay era was that we never found a replacement for Arlyn Bowers. Nolan's schemes demanded a smaller, dogged defender that could occasionally stick a three. That freed up Mayberry so he didn't have to guard the other team's point. It was hoped that Shephard could play that role as a juco transfer but he struggled.

Clint McDaniel was looked to as someone that could make a leap but had never played a lot. Corey Beck and Dwight Stewart were both juco transfers and we weren't sure what we were getting. They were both from Memphis. Corliss was of course the major hope of that team as an incoming freshman but he had broken his foot in the preseason and nobody knew if he would be ready for the opener.

So not only was our cupboard bare but Memphis State had beaten us twice in a row and they were now beating us for the best Memphis kids, Penny being the best example. Because that was the thing, Penny should have been OURS. We wanted him. We followed him in high school. At the time Memphis kids like Huery and Day were coming to US. And Penny was the next guard in that evolution. He was just that much better. He should have been OURS. It would have been SO PERFECT.

But that is how you make a good nemesis. And Penny was a great one. He dominated the first half, along with Vaughn. The hogs were tentative and confused and couldn't score to save their lives. If Penny wanted a jumper he just rose up and shot. On the break his vision was perfect and his passing deft. He could finish way above the rim.

Looking at the floor I just couldn't see where we were going to get points. A kid named Roger Crawford came in and looked like he had a little heart and Corliss was doing okay. But Dwight Stewart, who had been discussed as a possible replacement for Miller, came in and looked like a scared twelve year old with a hormone problem. I thought at the time that he would NEVER be a player.

At the half we were down something like 14 and it seemed like more. I went outside to smoke with a friend at halftime and we were bitterly depressed. We talked about how it was over, about how it was going to be a long season. We also talked about Penny.

I loved everything about Penny. I even loved his name. Anfernee Hardaway. His first name was like some sort of phonetic spelling of an Ebonic mispronounciation. EXCELLENT! That is the stuff legends are made of.

To this day Penny is the greatest basketball player I have ever seen in person and it's not really close. And I have seen a lot of great ones. I saw Bird but I was too young and too far away. But he was better than the Triplets or Mayberry and Day. Better than Olajuwan or Drexler or Shaq as college players. Better than Ricky Pierce or Vinny Johnson or Terry Teagle. Better than Alvin Robertson or Darrell Walker. I'm not talking about what any of them became. I'm talking about what they were in college.

My father says that Sprewell was close to Penny but I wasn't there for that Bama game. All I can tell you is what I saw. Nolan compared him to Magic, Bird and Jordan. At that age there really was nothing else to compare him to. He was actually a combination of those three. He nearly had the size of Magic and Bird. He was about 6'7". His passing was just a step below those two. His athleticism and penetration was way above either of them and just below Jordan. His shot was soft and natural and not as good as Bird but way better than Magic and a little better than Jordan. He could do EVERYTHING and he was unselfish and he saw the floor and he could bury the three. He wasn't a great defender but if he had played for Nolan he would have been.

In the end a million variables determine how good a player will become. How hard they work and whether their bodies hold up being two big factors. I have no idea how hard Penny worked. But his incredible body betrayed him just a couple years into the pros and it is truly sad. He was something to see. He was what you want from a nemesis.

I decided to use what might at first appear to be my weaknesses in my battle against the cardiologist. I am a sad, lonely, pathetic bachelor. And what are sad, lonely, pathetic bachelors good at? Exactly. Stalking via the internet. While he was helping the poor and homeless or showing his wife and children how much he loved them, I would be digging through the binary minutiae of his life. We would see who was the better man.

First I checked the registered sex offenders list for his name. No luck. It didn't prove anything as he could be breaking the law and not registering but even I have limits to how many state databases I'm willing to go through out of mere spite (4 it turns out). I turned my attention to published papers and court cases which of course led to his med school divorce and child custody dispute. A quick look at his phone number led me to his previous addresses and current occupants of those addresses and I found his ex-wife and a daughter. Life is so simple some times.

Date the ex-wife - as long as she isn't too much of a chubster.

The second half was a different story. I'm not sure what Nolan said to those guys but as far as I'm concerned he saved the program in that locker room. Well, the fact that David Vaughn blew out his knee in the second half and ruined his career to the extent that I don't think he ever started another game helped a little. Corliss looked great, if out of shape, in the second half. But at some point he re-injured his foot.

Somewhere around the 10 minute mark we became the team we would be for the next 2 years. Scotty Thurman, an unheralded recruit, hit a big shot or two. Roger Crawford buried a huge three. Robert Shephard was an ANIMAL as he would be the rest of the season. He was a steal MACHINE. Nobody slapped the ball and hands like Corey Beck, Robert Shephard and Clint McDaniel. At one point Memphis State just folded and quit. (Yes the great Penny had a touch of quit in him. That's why he should have come to play for US. He would've become a winner.)

The National Title team was born that day. The one moment in the second half that stands out the most came early. I still didn't know what to think of

Beck. He seemed kind of slow and maybe a little fat to me. He didn't shoot it and I wasn't sure what he brought to the table. Memphis always had one, sometimes two guys that were 6'5" muscled jumping jacks that could dunk but nothing else. They could rebound a little but were horrible shooters and mediocre defenders. They played more on their potential than anything else. Two or three times a game this guy would get an offensive rebound and throw it off the backboard so hard it wouldn't even draw iron. Think Larry Marks. Corey Beck was guarding that guy in the second half and they were talking smack back and forth. I figured it was the usual Memphis stuff. But the Hogs were way down and had just got stuffed again and the dude was talking and talking. So there was a break in the action for a second and the guy wasn't paying attention and Corey just walked up coolly and racked him. Punched him hard right in the 'nads. The guy bent over and Corey bent over with him and whispered something in his ear. The refs missed it. Everybody missed it. The guy never fought back and was quiet the rest of the game. He folded just like his team. It was a Godfather moment. I've loved Corey Beck ever since.

I always saw him as the manhood of Arkansas Basketball. The manhood we lost when Todd Day took that weak swing at Larry Johnson. And that game was the manhood of Arkansas Basketball. When we crushed our nemesis.

My nemesis was out cutting his grass. His two little boys were playing in battery powered jeeps. A beautiful 3 or 4 year old girl was playing on a swing set fancy enough to be in a park. The beautiful wife was trimming hedges. She was wearing shorts and had the body of a tennis pro.

I had checked out the ex-wife and found out she currently lived with a husky companion named Becca who wore cologne so my chances didn't look good. I was jogging by the cardiologist's house and my white and nearly hairless legs were blinding oncoming traffic. I was being taunted by guys in trucks as they drove by and my wind was so short I thought I would throw up at any moment. It was a beautiful Arkansas spring day. It smelled of honeysuckle and insecticide, fresh cut grass and dead squirrel.

I spied the happy cardiologist out of the corner of my blurring vision. I thought of Corey Beck. Somewhere I found a burst of energy and sprinted towards the heart man. He looked at me with bulging eyes as I gently pushed him. He tottered like a weeble then fell to the ground as I scurried back to my home.

I might need to find a new nemesis. I think this one is going to file charges.

A Mythology of Swine

The Wal-Mart Chronicles . . .

My nieces were asking me for a story. Well, sort of. The one I call Maddog was beating me about the head with a Nerf light saber and the one I call Boo was jumping on my shoulders until my arms went numb. The third one, the oldest, KiKi was the one asking for the story. She had reached the age of 11 and had less of a slapstick sensibility than the other two. Plus my nose was starting to bleed and she felt sorry for me. I always liked that KiKi.

My nieces like my stories. They like other things about me but that is what they like most. They like that I seem to lack discipline, I guess. That I like cartoons. That I am tall and can lift them up high. That I like video games and fart jokes. That I am fat and lazy and immensely enjoy naps. These things are endearing to children. But mostly they seem to like my stories. "Doctor Stories" or "Hawg Stories" they call them.

They live in Boston so I don't get to see them very much, 3 or 4 times a year maybe. This episode was Thanksgiving of last year, the Friday after the holiday actually, the day of the LSU game.

The stories that they like are, for the most part ones that involve me getting humiliated in some way. Or it could be my brother, or their mom. As long as somebody ends up looking like a complete idiot. They like to hear about how I would pick at my underwear when I was up at bat in pee-wee baseball. How my brother, as a fourth grader, stood on the foul line and told the entire crowd (and it was a surprisingly big crowd) to SHUT UP! so he could concentrate. They like hearing that I wore a speedo in age group swimming, but they cover their eyes when they hear it. Boo even gags a little. They like hearing me talk about ball games from when I was 16 like they still matter to anyone but me. They like missed buzzer shots and other guys getting the girl. Missed dunks and and my father caught on tape saying Holy S*** when my brother got in a game. This is the kind of mythology we are passing down in my family. A mythology for our nearly simpleminded tribe.

Before getting into the story for the night I needed to settle the girls into their beds which was troublesome for me. The nieces don't fear their Uncle Jay. Boo was drawing a picture of a horse on my shirt. Maddog was repeatedly dive-bombing me from the top bunk. And KiKi had stolen my cellphone to try and discover if any of her friends had stolen THEIR uncle's cell phones.

It seemed a combination of bribery and soft restraints worked best and eventually all were in bed and anxious to listen to their uncle. But they had some questions first.

"Are you still mad about the FOOTBALL game?" KiKi asked.

"Why do you yell so much when you watch sports?" Boo added. "It kinda scares me."

"What does f*** mean and why do you say it all the time when you watch football?" Maddog queried.

I decided to ignore Maddog, although she was now chanting the word in question and trying to rhyme it in made up songs.

I answered them the best way I knew how.

You see girls, your Uncle Jay is a sad, lonely, and pathetic man. The only things I have in my life are my family, my job, you guys and then whatever else I decide gives me a little joy. And sports does that.

Earlier this year I was in a bar by myself watching the Auburn football game. I wasn't in Arkansas so my shouts and yells seemed strange and out of place. But another guy there was following the game too. He grew up in Hot Springs and so we talked a little. I told him how McFadden reminded me a little bit of the way Eric Dickerson used to run. This guy had been at those games too He remembered Craig James and SMU's half-shirts. He remembered farther back and Earl Cambell in Fayetteville with his tear away jersey. He remembered basketball players like James Crockett with the sleepy eyes and Keenan Dubose with the Jerry-curl. Guys that never really became anything as players but are part of the fabric of things if you followed the teams closely.

I told the girls that I am at an age where I don't make friends any more. There is too much past to really connect with someone. But if there is a shared experience it changes things. If you like the same movies or music it is like you have known that person longer, shared more of a lifetime. I told them this is why I make them listen to Dylan and Steve Earle and Tom Waits and The Band. Why I make them dance with me barefoot on the deck on summer nights. It is about memory and shared experience. It is about creating a mythology to fall back on.

I told them that this is what sports is to me. That this is what Razorback sports is to our family. That it is a history filled with much success and much failure. It is an underdog's history and one to be proud of.

The girls were asleep now and I wasn't sure they heard any of my silly speech. I looked around their room. Clothes in piles. Books lined up next to clock radios. On the walls and ceiling were paw prints made by an imaginary green dog who stepped in a bucket of blue paint, mythology courtesy of Boo.

I don't know where the hatred and bile that currently consume the Arkansas football program would fall in it's history, or if I will tell my girls about FOIs and text messages, about death threats and police protection, about 18 year old boys exhalted and villified to such shocking extents the world must seem a very frightening place to them. It certainly makes for good stories but maybe not the kind I am interested in so much. I am more interested in the kid that runs like a young Eric Dickerson, or has a funky left handed jumper like Keenan Dubose.

The next morning my sister made pancakes and the girls and I were sucking down syrup and butter and Maddog was chanting her new, profane song as I told her to SHUSH!. My sister asked "Are you still depressed about the game Jay?"

KiKi and Boo answered in unison "Uncle Jay is a sad, lonely and pathetic man."

They left it at that.

Doctor Stories

Santa is Bleeding

Santa came into the ER on Christmas day. He didn't look so good.

People think I make this stuff up, and I guess sometimes I do. But I'm pretty sure this was real.

I didn't know it was him at first. He was showing some wear and tear. Checked in under an assumed name. All very understandable.

He had on some shiny new off-brand sneakers and overalls which was a little less so. I guess even Santa gets crummy presents from his grandkids and had to wear them to make them happy.

The beard had been white once but was now a tobacco stained yellow. His fingertips were swollen, curved, and brown from holding the cigarettes. There were also drips of juice matted in his facial hair from a dip he kept in his mouth. Santa was a nicotine junky.

Spidery veins snaked across his nose, the skin weathered from a life outdoors, the pores big and tired. His eyes didn't sparkle. They kind of popped out of his head. I'm pretty sure Santa had a thyroid problem.

He didn't talk much, but his voice was low and throaty. He cleared phelgm on a subconscious level. There were no "ho, ho, hos". He belched a lot though. It smelled like rotten ham.

Santa was having chest pain, not an unusual complaint on Christmas day. For the sake of our medical system families should generally not gather together. It doesn't work out too well. Lots of chest pain, lots of domestic violence, lots of anxiety and stomach trouble. Santa was no exception. His family had dragged him in.

The family was a bit of a surprise though. No elves. The daughter went about 350. Mrs. Claus appeared to be a fairly recent Philipine import. She had a bad complexion and a surly attitude and smoked like a chimney. I kind of had a thing for her.

Santa's chest pain had actually been coming and going for awhile, getting worse with the increased workload of the season. More of a shoulder tightness than anything, his arm would go numb to the elbow. He was feeling better now and wanted to go home. His EKG looked alright and I told him that if his bloodwork was normal and he insisted on going home we could work something out. Santa just belched again. It was fishier this time. Like something had died inside him.

In fact something had died inside him. A tiny little piece of his heart. Santa's cardiac enzymes were elevated. This, together with the fact that he had a normal

EKG and his symptoms were gone meant that he'd had a small heart attack (a non-q wave or subendocardial MI) the night before or early that morning while he was doing you know what. I told him all of this and he was cool about it. Asked if he could smoke. I told him the plan - anticoagulants, betablockers, a transfer to a cardiologist (by sleigh if necessary) for an eventual cardiac cath and the likely findings when they did that (small vessel disease - unknown whether the large vessels involved, likely multivessel, possible bypass, blah blah blah).

Santa decided that this was a good time to tell me he had Lupus. I suppose it didn't make any difference to me now and the lack of knowledge hadn't affected the workup but it always amazes me what exactly people think I mean when I ask if they have ANY HEALTH PROBLEMS AT ALL. That perhaps that could include chronic, inflammatory, life threatening illnesses that affect every organ in the body. And it appeared he had never been treated for this either, or at least followed since he didn't have a doctor. In the short time I had known him I had decided that Santa didn't always make the wisest choices.

Lupus is one of the great diseases and it was recognized in an era when diseases got great names. It comes from the the same Latin root as Lupine or "wolflike". In the simplest terms Lupus is an auto-immune disease. The body's immune system begins mistaking its own tissues for foreign substances and attacks them by binding to them with antibodies. Bad things ensue. Rashes, kidney inflammation and failure, diabetes, heart inflammation and coronary disease, paradoxically compromised immune system, and multiple infections. It can be mild or devastating. It can look like anything or nothing. I'm not sure why they called the disease "the Wolf" when they first described it. Maybe it was that the butterfly shaped facial rash that many victims get looks vaguely wolflike. I like to think it's because the disease itself seems smart and mean. Coming in the night, under cover of darkness to take your hope and your soul. Killing you slowly, inevitably. Perhaps they saw it as the devil himself.

I didn't want to yell at Santa for not telling me he had Lupus. He was just like everybody else. He didn't understand or wasn't paying attention or was just scared. Or maybe he preferred to ignore and minimize the fact that he had this disease. Did it so well that he had forgotten.

It didn't matter. Doesn't matter. It's all the same anyway. Santa is okay for now. He will be for awhile. But he is slowly wearing away. Being eaten from the inside. Chewed up by none other than himself. By his own dual nature. It doesn't matter if we spend our lives bringing joy to the world, bringing peace for a night. In the end the Wolf comes. He is just waiting inside us.

Thursday Night

The Wal-Mart Chronicles . . .

There is an unspeakable perfection to an empty ER. My ER is small and so it is a small perfection. A janitor comes through to empty trash cans. A security guard plays solitaire on the computer. A skinny guy in a hospital gown with an IV pole and fuzzy slippers wanders through looking for a place to smoke. Buzz, an EMT, has on headphones, working on some kind of music mix. Tom, a paramedic, is reading a book about the Indonesian sex trade. Mike, an R.N., is working on his charts. I'm just sitting on my stool, wishing someone would talk to me.

"How's the book Thomas?" I ask.

"I want to move to Indonesia." he says. "They seem so civilized about sexual perversity over there."

"Yeah." I'm nodding. " Rather draconian with the drug laws though."

"It seems like a contradiction", Tom says, stroking his goatee in a thoughful manner. " I mean, it seems like you'd want to get good and f****d up before you had sex with children."

"At least after", I say. " For the shame and all."

Tom just nods and goes back to reading.

"What about bestiality?" I ask.

"What about it?"

"Is there a lot of that or just the pedophilia?"

"I'm sure there's a lot of that but its not covered in this book. I don't think those guys are quite ready to join hands and acknowledge their proclivities yet. I think Germany is the place with the most sophisticated bestiality."

"Sophisticated bestiality?" I ask, remarking that this would be a good album title. Tom ignores me.

"It involves large animals" he says. " Big dogs. Great Danes and such. There also seems to be quite a bit of stuff going on over there with bodily functions. Corporophasia or corporophagia I think they call it. I'm not sure. Not really my thing. The porn and sex industry have gone much further in Germany and in Eastern Europe than they have here. Eastern European porn is definitely cutting edge. Over here its much quieter, more conventional. The love between a man and his animal is a quiet one.

I nod. Pleased with Tom's wisdom on the subject. Comforted that someone I know is keeping up.

Mike starts banging his head on the desk in a slow and steady manner. The ambulance phone rings. F***! we all say in unison.

What Teef?

She came in by ambulance, because that's how they come. After the kind of ass kicking you read about in books and hear about in songs but only a certain segment of the population ever really sees. A good solid real life DV beating. Domestic violence in all its glory and there isn't a goddam thing domestic about it. It is raw and untamed and seems to be about three steps backwards on the evolutionary scale. It strikes me as being something apart. As being "other".

That's one of the things about it though, about the ass kicking and about evolution. It's not "other" and it's not apart and it has nothing to do with progress. Evolution is simply changes selected by pressures. It has nothing to do with "improvements" and "progress". We are nothing but a bunch of zigs and zags and lateral moves from the chimps and lions. Suckling our young, masturbating in public, and beating the living fuck out of people in wild rages.

She came in by ambulance, because that's how they come. These matted haired DVs with their bowed heads and swollen eyes. She was quiet and she cut looks back and forth, watching the perimeter. She stunk. She stunk of poverty and rape and dirt and hand me downs and meth labs and years of hopelessness. The hopelessness has a smell all its own. But mostly she stunk of booze, sour and cheap. It oozed from her pours and gave her breath an edge that melted plastic. One more thing she seemed ashamed of.

I tried to look at her face. It looked asian or mongoloid because of the swelling. Her upper lip fat and her right eye oozing bloody tears from a torn duct. Her nose flat like a boxer's or maybe Hedda Nussbaum's if you saw those pictures. A face fractured too many times to repair itself. It just quits and lays there.

She flinches every time I try to touch her face. The flinch doesn't extinguish, doesn't go away even when she knows I won't hurt her. She acts like old patients with dementia and chronic brain damage to their frontal lobes. She won't hold still. She just wants to leave. I ask her if her teeth hurt, if she lost any. What teef? she says.

She came in by ambulance, because that's how they come and she left alone with a friend. Three fractures to her face. She asked me if I thought she was stupid for putting up with this shit and I told her I wasn't sure. I was picturing her in my head just laying there, taking the beating from an enraged drunk, just taking it. Flinching about as much as she flinched when I touched her. Not even bothering to put her arms up to protect her face any more. I asked her if it was scary, just laying there when the fists came down like that. Yeah, she said. Sometimes it's scary.

She came in by ambulance, because that's how they come. I'm starting to wonder why we give them names.

Army of the Angry Plain

The Wal-Mart Chronicles . . .

One of my girls rolled in. Actually a young woman, 23, but they all seem like girls to me now. Stuck in some kind of permanent adolesence, a relentless, awkward torment of the soul.

I hadn't seen this one before. Her boyfriend was carrying her. She had passed out after drinking a bunch of vodka and taking some xanax. He left her for awhile and when he came back he could barely wake her up. They looked like college dropouts. He seemed nice enough. I assume he was lying at least a little bit. I would be.

After we got her in a bed and had an IV and we did our thing with tubes and catheters and charcoal and tox screens and alcohol levels and made sure she would be okay, she woke up and talked a bit. She was drunk and slurry and kept asking where she was but for the most part was OK. Boyfriend guy tells us she ODed before - after an abortion and he was a little concerned about depression.

We seem to have one of these a week. Its the faces on these girls that strike me. There is a remarkable homogeneity to them. An underclass of the not quite pretty - an army of the angry plain. Their faces have acne scars or marks from a car accident or something else that will never be repaired. The damage to their souls is right there for the world to see. People must whisper behind them "She'd be so pretty except" except she wouldn't be. She wears caked make up to cover the scars and any character her face might have is smothered, literally choked for air. Dark mascara, always running with tears when I see them, like sad clowns. Chipped teeth and weak chins. I can just see them in the back of a tenth grade classroom, willing to get drunker and go down on more guys to get some attention. I assume they all learned this was the way of the world at a much younger age. That is the kind of knowledge that doesn't wash off. These are my OD girls. And that is what this one looks like too.

She's wearing hip hugger jeans and a half shirt with a belly ring and a cheap tattoo of a bird flying into her waistband. She is too chunky for the oufit but not by much. She has missed everything in this life by a fraction it seems. Her boyfriend steps out and she wants to talk. She is flat on her back and looking up at me, apologizing for her slurred speech, almost whispering. She does a thing that they all seem to do. She reaches a hand out and starts rubbing my arm as she talks, their is something unmistakably flirty, sexual in the way they look at me. They can't help themselves, all encounters with men have become sexual somehow.

The worst part, and maybe the most revealing, is that on some level I seem to like it - this weird attention from the scrap heap of emotional need.

This one is Anna and she pukes again but then starts back flirting. There is no connection in her brain that one should discourage the other. She whispers that this isn't where she thought she would wake up. She uses her fingers to brush back her vomit stained hair.

I don't make the connection right away. I think she means that she expected to wake up at home or in another bed. She seems spooked.

She says that she has tried this many times before and it is very scary and how many times does she have to try it. She says she is sorry she can't talk right. She rubs my arm again and dry heaves. She wants to go to sleep and be done with this world. She hints that she thought she would wake up in hell.

Anna tells me she is Brazilian, apparently by way of Texas for a generation or so, and she seems to think that this explains her views on things. How many times? she asks me again. Its the fear that grips her as she is falling asleep. She wants me to understand the courage it takes to try. She says she doesn't know if she can keep doing it.

Her fiance came back and, after advising him to run far, far away from this chick, we talked a bit more about her past.

It had been 3 abortions. All in the past 2 years. And the Brazilian family is very Catholic. He says that she is not religious.

It can be cool how a religion can gnaw at you and cause guilt and grief long after you have rejected it. Pope's and priests everywhere tormenting women from afar then condemning them to eternal fire.

But its all good for me. I get to see them in their flawed and smeared glory. And maybe the ugliest thing of all - for some reason they always seem to cheer me up a little.

The End

About the Author

Mr. Kradel is an ER doctor in Arkansas and has been for the past 11 years. He leads a meaningless existence, obsessed with college basketball and more importantly his beloved Arkansas Razorbacks.

He has completed one novel but it was really bad and frankly kind of silly. He is working on another but given his track record hopes aren't high.

www.ingramcontent.com/pod-product-compliance
Lightning Source LLC
LaVergne TN
LVHW091642100826
845152LV00006B/139/J
* 9 7 8 0 5 7 8 0 0 7 9 3 9 *